"THANKSGIVING BY ACTION!"

INVOCATIONS

THE AUTHOR

Harold J. (Bud) Palmer grew up in Mt. Vernon, NY
and graduated, with a BBA and MBA from

Pace University, NY.

He has been married to Angela Wojdak from Scranton,
PA since 1986. Bud has 5 children and 16 grandchildren
scattered throughout the Eastern US.

Work consisted of ownership of The Palmer Group, a Manufacturer's Rep. firm in
Wyckoff, NJ. After moving to Florida full time in 2006, he joined Marco Island Sunrise
Rotary in 2009, served as President in 2012-2013 as well as various other positions. Bud
was named Rotarian of the Year for 2020-2021 and provides this reference book as his
"encore" for that award. He is a previous Amazon #1 Best Selling Author.

DEDICATION

To compile this reference book, I have come to realize that all that we do
in Rotary is a prayer. A prayer of : "Thanksgiving by Action"!

Ubi Caratas est vera, Deus ebi est.
"Where charity is true, God himself is there".

Rotary is unique in that as a benevolent organization, it is unified in only helping others.
It is so effective that closed societies such as Communist states do not permit Rotary to
exist within their borders. This is because they cannot control them. To their people's
detriment.

"If we can help but one child our life will be fulfilled". Therefore, I dedicate this volume to
our Rotary "Gift of Life" effort to repair little hearts and allow the least of these, the
children, to enjoy childhood as other children do and grow to faith and prosperity.

TABLE OF CONTENTS

INTRODUCTION

Paul Harris said: "Whatever Rotary may mean to us, to the world it will be known by the results it achieves."

Rotary asks us to perform "Service Above Self". We are all aware of the analogy: not to "hide under a bushel basket". I suppose the true term is" Discipleship". In this sense, we are required to work in His service.

Rotary has shown me and given me the opportunity to come "out of the closet" of faith complacency.

If "A closed mind is the mother of ignorance",

it is born, fostered and nurtured to be ignorant by its very nature and definition. Rotary, in many ways, opens our minds to the treasure of helping others.

What then of the open mind? We are but compilers of information. So, the question: where do we arrange that in our intellect?

Our influences are many and diverse. When we get to a certain age, it gets easier to reject bad influences and accept the good and meaningful. God, country, family, community combine to define what is important. They are time tested. Changes and forces outside ourselves somehow develop into a mindset to give back. If we can but reach beyond ourselves. Rotary offers the vehicle to do just that. Give back!

If not for the holy spirit, who then? How do you compose from nothing to something that is meaningful to a group of people? What happens that presents something in writing that is coherent and makes sense to a group?

There were many times when I had nothing and had to copy something from a past invocation. There were times when an event, speaker, a program or cause outlined what was necessary. Other times when my attitude was, Oh well! Let's get it done. However, there were many times when I just sat down and wrote. Somehow it wasn't me. This book is both a confession and atonement to raise myself to a level where I can, in some small way, give back.

Since my Club Presidency in 2012-2013 I have been blessed to take over writing invocations for our club. Before that year we had a list of prayers that pertained to various programs and events. My assessment was that it was limiting, and without inspiration. That is, not seeing what was current in the world: our society, and events relative to our club and community. Things change, and to refresh, we needed our invocations to introduce the meeting and speaker as well as programs and service that our club wanted. I felt the invocation should set the tone for the meeting. It became a meetings introduction as well as a prayer invoking Almighty God and the Holy Spirit to give us the ability to absorb His grace in our meeting. We are obliged to sanctify Rotary meetings and our work simply because God has sanctified us to do that work. There is a certain power in His inspiration that makes that work more meaningful. Better for all concerned.

Why not? After all God gives us the ability and He challenges His people to perform Rotary's mission.

Somehow, I wonder, I was chosen as Rotarian of the Year in 2020-2021. The question then was: "what do I do for an encore"? We have, collectively, the intelligence and the ability to create real passion for meaningful causes to improve lives, I had the material so I jumped in to create this volume. I hope and pray that we may all benefit, especially the children through "Gift of Life."

You may note from the invocations in this reference the absence of Jesus, The Christ. My personal opinion is that Jesus is certainly the Word of God and the Second Person of the Holy Trinity. However, this book is not for me. It is for Rotary and Rotarians. Our clubs are comprised of many faiths and there are various conceptions of Jesus as our Lord and Savior. To invoke Jesus can be disrespectful faithfully to them, but it is also considerate of those other faiths and, hopefully, an inclusive atmosphere in our club (forgive me for my justification). The user of this compilation of prayer is properly able to insert whatever text is appropriate to the audience as long as it is a prayer invoking God.

I have tried to organize these works by community and world events with Rotary projects and programs applying the Rotary principals:

"Service Above Self"

"The Four Way Test"

And, If the readers take the time, they will see certain invocations repeated for more than one category. The reasoning behind this repetition is to provide an easier reference for those that are looking to use an invocation for a certain purpose.

ROTARY AREAS OF FOCUS

Polio Plus
Promote Clean Water and Sanitation
Peace and Conflict Resolution
Health and Disease Prevention
Fight Illiteracy and Poverty
The Environment
Child and Maternal Health
Disaster Response

Where there is hunger and poverty there are Rotarians.
Where there are weather disasters there are Rotarians.
Where education is needed there are Rotarians.
Where health problems exist Rotarians volunteer.

Conflict resolution causes Rotarians to volunteer because we believe in
"Peace thru Service".
This compilation of prayer has been a labor of love and growth and a means of giving
back to the cross-section of Rotarians I have met. All have contributed to my personal
growth and this work has a little bit of every Rotarian in it. Rotary is greater than the sum
of its parts, hence this reference book.

Let us Pray!
Almighty God, as Rotarians You have challenged us to act together and see a world where
people unite and take action to create lasting improvement in the lives of others.
Across the globe: in our communities, and in ourselves, our neighbors and our friends, we
ask for Your guidance to take action to create lasting change. We ask by Your Grace, that
we pour our passion, integrity, and intelligence into completing projects that have a
lasting impact.
May we persevere until we deliver real, lasting solutions to create lasting change.
We pray to remember Rotary history. For well over 100 years, Rotarians have bridged
cultures and connected continents to champion peace, fight illiteracy and poverty,
promote clean water and sanitation, and fight disease.
We pray for Your continued grace!
Amen.

1. SERVICE ABOVE SELF

No Greater Love.

District Meeting 5/13/18
Let us pray!
"A greater love hath no man than to lay down his life for a friend".
Rotarians are seldom called to this extreme measure, but we welcome the challenge to give of ourselves to serve others.
We do not look upon ourselves or our fellow Rotarians as hero's. Rotarians give "Service Above Self" because we only wish to share some of how You have blessed us.
If we have been blessed with knowledge - Rotarians share that knowledge.
If You have given us talent - Rotarians share that talent. Rotarians are willing to give whatever they can beyond what we need.
We observe what is good, what is true, and what is beautiful to improve education, repair and restore health, resolve conflicts and promote peace because we know that it pleases You, our God.
All of us are equal in Your eyes and only need the chance to develop our fellow citizens as we have been blessed. We ask that You bestow Your grace upon us and all Rotarians to remember what You have given us to give to others.
In Thy name we pray!
Amen.

Paul Harris.

Let us Pray:
As Paul Harris said:
"Whatever Rotary may mean to us, to the world it will be known by the results it achieves."
Help us, O Lord, to fulfill the projects we now are engaged in that their achievement will be pleasing to you. We pray that our human service, from one person to another, and from this club to the health and well being of others, may always reflect Your love and mercy in this world.
Amen.

Human Spirit.

Let us Pray;

Almighty God,

We are thankful that You have given us the 7 great attributes of the human spirit:
First, Our Body: as a tabernacle of Your design to nourish and maintain at
maximum health.

Our heart: the center of our being distributing more than life giving fluid and
nourishment, but containing our faith and trust in You to absorb and feel
regeneration of Your will for us.

Our mind: that dwells on the importance of giving of ourselves to others

Our memory: of the vast amalgam of learning and experience of so many that
have done Your work through Rotary

Our intellect: to clarify. When combined with other Rotarians we dynamically
produce projects that are good, true and beautiful for a better world.

Our will: and desire to enthusiastically generate unselfish improvements to the
social order.

And finally: our soul which reflects who we are and how we are recognized as
Rotarians.

In thy name we pray, Amen.

The Narrow Gate

Let us Pray!

Almighty God, as Rotarians enter the "Narrow Gate" of "Service Above Self" we ask for
Your grace and guidance as we formulate plans and programs to help others.

We understand that "Resting on our Laurels" is only a baseline for our progress.

We pray that we may re-energize our giving and go down that "road less traveled" to a
future of better health and resolution of conflicts for our world community.

Guide us, o Lord in giving "Peace thru Service".

In thy name we pray,

Amen.

Not Alone.

Let us pray!

Almighty God, as we make our way through this life we sometimes need
to be awakened from our own problems to finally realize that we long to
see your face and are not alone.

As we are accustomed to our comfortable life in paradise, there are others,
Rotarians work to reach, that require assistance for the very basics in life.
As we practice to understand their plight we ask for Your guidance and
grace to truly understand their needs.

We pray that Rotarians work in harmony that we may assist those in need.

In thy name we pray!

Amen

Ultimate Refuge.

Let us Pray!

Almighty God,

We pray to You to erase the fear and tension between people.

We realize that You are our ultimate refuge for our own consolation. Please bring that
consolation to others engaged in disturbing the tranquility of our nation. We pray that
they seek in You the true meaning of fellowship that all Rotarians enjoy.

We pray that the present suffering be rectified and then rejuvenated with the American
spirit of cooperation and sanctity known as *"charity for all"*.

We pray that minds and hearts be overcome with a willingness and dedication to serve
others and provide improvement in others welfare before their own.

With heartfelt love of You, our God, penetrate all with the generous gifts You have given
us.

In thy name we pray,

Amen.

Humility.

Let Us Pray!

It is right and just that You have given Rotarians Your Spirit to discern and implement the very natural promise mankind must achieve.

With humility, - - - Rotarians accept the work of a very personal organization in Your name.

We are a movement of many minds, cultures and beliefs that transcend individual motives and understand that the one, common purpose joining Rotarians is performing in Your name.

The depth of "Service Above Self" is the idea that we must search our soul and rise above personal interests to achieve peace, justice and a world where all are without the encumbrance of poverty - - - through our Service.

Amen!

Peace

Let us Pray;

Almighty God, at this time of year we pray especially for the core Rotary effort of peace and the resolution of conflicts throughout the world.

We hold great hope for the future of our great country and, in unison, we wish to join with others to promote Your principals in the joy of charity for all.

We pray that all here continue to put "service above self" and guide our efforts with enthusiasm for Rotary and our fellow citizens throughout the world.

Amen.

Joy of Service

Let us Pray!
To give anonymously is the greatest satisfaction.
As You, our Lord, guides us through our everyday lives, we pray to be, meekly,
last - that we may be first in Your kingdom.
By Rotarians serving others before self, we pray to maintain humility in giving of
our time, talent and treasure.
The true joy we receive - is the only reward we seek.
Lord, you who have given us the gifts of discernment and discretion to conduct
our Rotary and everyday lives.
Work through us to prudently discover the goodness in others and especially
goodness in our fellow Rotarians.
We pray that we may trust each others judgement as we work together to give our
talents and treasures for the betterment of our community and for a world living
the Rotarian principals of truth, fairness, benefit and goodwill to all concerned.
Amen.

Fellowship

Let us Pray!
May those assembled here today enjoy the many offerings of Rotary.
May we abide by the rules we have established: those of trust, fellowship and ethics, and
may we place "Service Above Self" in our daily endeavors.
May we always test ourselves and our efforts to be sure they are the truth, good for all
concerned, of benefit to mankind, and provide peace and understanding.
Amen.

Time, Talent and Treasure

Let us Pray!

Almighty God, heavenly father, we are here to serve.
We are humbled by the need for help by so many. As a Rotary Club we
have endeavored to discover where we can help and proceeded to
implement programs to assist our fellows.
The heartwarming co-operation and help from all with their time, talent
and treasure propels us all into a new year of hope.
With faith in You, hope that we can project whatever we have to others,
and the charity built into the human soul by You, our God, we pray for
Your guidance and care moving forward into a new Rotary year.
In thy name we pray,
Amen

The Higher Good

Let us Pray!

We pray that you help us and all Rotarians to attain the higher good.
As those Rotarians before us, we respect the programs that have
evolved over the past 100 years.
We struggle, O Lord, with the hierarchy of the good we do in our lives.
We pray that our choices be for the higher good and that we can resolve, with our
families, and with ourselves any issues that may hold us back from attaining that higher
good and living the life of Rotary.
Amen

Recollection

Let Us Pray!

Dear Lord, as we gather in assembly, we pray to You to instill in us the best of intentions in fulfilling Rotary ideals.

We have no problem in remembering the: "Four Way Test" or "Service Above Self" when we are assembled here.

As You are aware, it sometimes becomes difficult to remember those messages in our daily activities.

We pray that You be with us perpetually, as counsel, as we go thru everyday life because Your principals are Rotary principals.

Amen.

Unalienable Rights

Let us Pray!

Almighty God, we, in America, have developed from the Unalienable Rights of Your providence with the freedoms written into our Constitution.

By inshrining our Freedoms of Speech, Religion, Assembly and Press we enjoy Life and liberty as Your legacy.

You have blessed America with abundance well beyond what our founders envisioned.

We pray that we, as Rotarians, continue to pass on this heritage to all the world with "Service Above Self."

In thy name we pray,

Amen

Personal Quest

Let us pray:
It is right and just that You have given Rotarians Your Spirit to discern and
implement the very natural promise mankind must achieve.
With humility, - - - Rotarians accept the work of a very personal
organization in Your name.
We are a movement of many minds, cultures and beliefs that transcend
individual motives and understand that the one, common purpose joining
Rotarians is performing in Your name.
The depth of "Service Above Self" is the idea that we must search our soul and
rise above personal interests to achieve Peace, justice and a world where all are
without the encumbrance of poverty - - - through our Service.
Amen!

Transcending Boundaries

Let us pray;
Almighty God, our feeling for our salvation and living with You, now and
in the future, is our goal. As our faiths merge and coincide in service to
You, we pray that they re-merge in service to others.
Rotarians transcend national boundaries, cultures and religious
orientation as a way of performing Your will that we may serve "the least
of these" in their need.
We pray to continue in this great joy of giving with Your inspiration in
this Holy time.
In thy name we pray!
Amen.

Peace thru Service

Let us pray,
Almighty God, Heavenly Father
we pray as we maintain communion with each other in common cause
and take inspiration from our motto: "Service Above Self".
As our Communion of Rotary like minds and spirit are being tested, as are
all those subject to severe health concerns, we take solace knowing
You have given us the ability to adapt creatively to socially distance
ourselves from each other. We know that You are with us in communion
without distance.
As we endeavor to embrace all those with health hardships and, as we
make the best of the Burden of Separation from each other, we reflect on
not being separated from You. We gather inspiration and hope
as we muster Rotarian talents and abilities to persevere under difficult
circumstances. Our hope in communion with You can only make
Rotarians stronger in our dedication for "Peace thru Service".
In thy name we pray,
Amen.

A Small Pebble

Let us pray!
Almighty God, we pray for the tranquility and peace in knowing You, our
God.
A small pebble can disturb the tranquility of a pond.
As we struggle to recover and overcome our present disturbance, let us
proceed with caution as a "small pebble" for good as we promote our
positive creed: "Service Above Self".
As we pray, our thoughts are consumed with You and Your will for us
knowing that much good ofter comes from tragedy.
We pray that Rotary spirit/ be energized for others to do good and **serve** in
order to bring a higher level of peace and understanding.
In thy name we pray,
Amen.

Christmas

Let is Pray;
Lord, as we celebrate the birth of our lord and savior, we pray to remember his word that we may follow with those words and the word of our motto:
"Service above Self".
As You gave Your son to us, we pray to continue collectively to present those principles to others and project them with the joy that comes through to the love You have given to us.
As we translate Your love into charity and giving in this season, we pray that others will join us to keep You in Christmas.
Amen.

Discernment

Let us Pray;
O Lord, You have given us the ability to discern, first, what is important to You in our daily lives.
We have accepted Rotary as the vehicle before us that fulfills Your desire for us to perform charitable giving on a local and in a worldwide effort.
As Rotarians, we understand our small part in combining with others to faithfully execute our and Your duties.
We have pledged, by the four way test, to Service Above Self with diligence and fidelity to Your Word.
Amen.

Discernment

Let Us Pray!
It is right and just that You have given Rotarians Your Spirit to discern
and implement the very natural promise mankind must achieve.
With humility, - - - Rotarians accept the work of a very personal
organization in Your name.
We are a movement of many minds, cultures and beliefs that transcend
individual motives and understand that the one, common purpose joining
Rotarians is performing in Your name.
The depth of "Service Above Self" is the idea that we must search our soul
and rise above personal interests to achieve Peace, justice and a world
where all are without the encumbrance of poverty - - - through our
Service.
Amen!

Doing Unto Others

Let us Pray;
As Rotarians we follow Your call, Almighty God, to go beyond "doing
unto others as we would have done to us".
By adopting the core principle: "Service Above Self" Rotarians are
committed to go beyond caring, or concern or empathy.
With compassion for others less fortunate we pray for Your Grace and
Guidance by performing.
Performing to provide services for: Peace and Conflict Resolution, Health
and Disease Prevention, Clean Water and Education among other core
programs to create lasting change.
"Service above Self" for Rotarians means compassion and performance
for others.
In thy name we pray,
Amen.

New Members

Let us pray!
As we embrace others that find in their hearts a willingness to serve others
we remember your charge to us to humbly accept all who find that
"Service Above Self" fulfills your will.
For those that are joining Rotary efforts to serve others we wish to accept
whatever fresh and innovative help and new thinking help Rotary efforts
to improve others lives.
As a Rotary family, we pledge to work with our new members in their
interests to serve You thru Rotary.
We pray for unity of purpose and dedication to Your will for all Rotarians.
In thy name we pray,
Amen.

Rotary Family

Let us pray,
You have guided Rotarians through great challenges in the past year.
Through it all we have adapted and planned anew to serve beyond the
normal call to duty. Our strength comes from You. Our dedication is built
into the character You provide Rotarians.
We recall our natural families and how You have given us the natural
transmission of heredity to produce more fruitful and dedicated members
of our *personal* community.
As a *chosen* community, we pray that we can give Rotary those familial
talents and willingness to make a better world. May we find the peace and
joy of our personal family in our Rotary family.
In thy name we pray,
Amen.

Sheltering in Place

Let us pray,
Almighty God, heavenly father, we are in awe and amazement at Your
power to provide Rotarians with the ability to perform important work for
the betterment of mankind. Even in a time of crisis when most are
"Sheltered in Place" and their own welfare may be in jeopardy.
The intellect, and will to use the abilities You have given us to help those
in need, is manifest in navigating the complexities of securing and
building funds under the Rotary Foundation. We are thankful for the
pouring out of Your grace and inspiration.
Although our local fundraising is temporarily curtailed by a hidden
enemy, we pray to continue to seek assistance from wherever it may be
found and to use Your grace as our guide for "Service Above Self".
In thy name we pray,
Amen.

Social Distance

Let us pray,
Almighty God, Heavenly Father
we pray as we maintain communion with each other in common cause
and take inspiration from our motto: "Service Above Self".
As our Communion of Rotary like minds and spirit are being tested, as are
all those subject to severe health concerns, we take solace knowing
You have given us the ability to adapt creatively to socially distance
ourselves from each other. We know that You are with us in communion
without distance.
As we endeavor to embrace all those with health hardships and, as we
make the best of the Burden of Separation from each other, we reflect on
not being separated from You. We gather inspiration and hope
as we muster Rotarian talents and abilities to persevere under difficult
circumstances. Our hope in communion with You can only make
Rotarians stronger in our dedication for "Peace thru Service".
In thy name we pray,
Amen.

Elections

Let us Pray!
Almighty God, we praise You and thank you for blessing us to live in this
sweet land of liberty and freedom to exercise our ability to choose.
With the ability You have given us to project Your will with our heart, our
mind and our intellect we pray for outcomes that will continue Your will
for us and for our individual freedom.
As we elect individuals to project Your and our will, we pray that You
bless them with the conviction and ability to defend Rotarian principals of
"Service Above Self" and "Fairness to All Concerned".
In thy name we pray,
Amen.

Inspiration

Let us pray;
Almighty God,
Two quotations come to mind:
The first: "Faith, Hope and Love. And the greatest of these is Love."
The second:
"With Malice toward none and Charity for all" as expressed in our history
and in our hearts as Americans and Rotarians.
This hope for mankind is given to us by Your grace.
The implications of Hope implies promise, but also risk and taking us out
of our comfort zone for Rotarians to advance the human condition.
Our gift is American exceptionalism and our promise is to spread the
Rotary message of hope and charity for all: with dedication and sacrifice to
give unselfishly, and to perform Your will as Faith in you gives us the
comfort of hope for those in need.
As Rotarians rally together to help our fellow citizens, we remain forever
in Your debt for the inspiration to perform "Service Above Self" with a
firm grip on Hope.
In thy name we pray,
Amen.

Rotarians as Examples

Service Above Self
Almighty God, our hope is in you.
We take to heart your abundant grace and invocation to
us, Your people, to use our hearts and minds to promote Rotary
principles.
Among the principles is "Service Above Self".
We understand that it is one thing to live this principle, but quite another
to speak to others and promote what we live and believe.
Please, Oh Lord, endow Rotarians with the ability to use what You have
taught us to be true in our conversations with others, in our
correspondence and in our daily encounters.
We pray that demonstrably speaking the truth of "Service Above Self"
become evident in our actions that we will have no fear in voicing our
actions and speech.
We pray that voicing our actions become infectious in a world much in
need of giving to others.
In thy name we pray,
Amen.

Clarity of Action

Let us pray,
We cast our worries before You o Lord with humility. We pray that You
illuminate our hearts and minds with the clarity only You can provide.
From Your Heavenly Sanctuary work in our lives, although we may be remote
from each other knowing that You are not remote from us.
Perhaps we have been lulled into a complacent place that threatens our
worship of You.
Perhaps we have been distracted by things not essential to our faith in You.
Shower Rotarians with Your grace, sanctify us in the gifts You have given us.
As we re-appraise our personal values and Renew our sense of purpose, may we
now long for closeness to You.
In thy name we pray,
Amen.

Public Servants

Service Above Self

Almighty God, we praise you and thank you for our public servants. Folks that train and work for others in need everyday performing "Service Above Self". We thank our first responders for always being present to sacrifice in emergency, but also being ever-present in our community for assistance as needed. Our public servants first respond to our call and volunteer their time, facilities and equipment to enhance our welfare and sense of community their experience , time, facilities. Our first responders bring public service to a higher level and bring the community together in the spirit of Your love for us. We pray, as a community of Rotarians, that in this season of salvation and love for each other, their service becomes an inspiration for the next generation to serve.

In thy name we pray,

Amen.

Projects

Let us Pray!

Almighty God, as Rotarians take action locally and globally each day, we ask Your guidance for our members as we pour our passion, integrity, and intelligence into completing projects that have a lasting impact. We pray to persevere until we deliver real, lasting solutions as we bridge cultures and connect continents to champion peace, fight illiteracy and poverty, promote clean water and sanitation, and fight disease.

In Thy name we pray,

Amen.

Good Counsel

Let Us Pray!

Dear Lord, we pray to You to instill in us the best of intentions
in fulfilling Rotary ideals.

We have no problem in remembering the: "Four Way Test" or "Service
Above Self". You know we repeat it often enough in our weekly meetings.
As You are also aware, it sometimes becomes difficult to remember those
messages in our daily activities.

We pray that You be with us perpetually, as counsel, as we go thru
everyday life because Your principals are Rotary principals.

Amen.

2. FOUR WAY TEST

Virtues

Let Us Pray!

O Lord, in our daily application of the "Four Way Test" grant us:

The virtues of patience to

Prudently discern others points-of-view,

Temperance to thoughtfully explain our position, and

To impart **Justice** with the

Fortitude Your grace gives us.

Grant us the vision of **Faith,**

The inspiration of **Hope,** and

The blessings of **Charity.**

Amen.

Freedom and Choice

Let us Pray!

Oh Lord we pray for the American ideals of: "Liberty and Justice for All".

As Rotarians we embrace liberty as the freedom and choice to decide as individuals to follow the principals You have set down for us and we record them as the Rotary principals in the Four Way Test.

We respect others as they follow their own desires to improve their community and pray that we may alway cooperate in our joint efforts.

We pray that we may justly come together to accomplish our common goals.

Amen.

Judgement

Let us Pray;

As Rotarian, we ask, oh Lord, for you guidance in helping us fulfill the Four Way Test. As we take on projects and donations, help us to discern Your judgement as you come into our heart, our mind, our memory, our intellect and our will to help others in our community and in our Rotary world.

Amen.

Service Above Self

Let us Pray;

O Lord, You have given us the ability to discern, first, what is important to You in our daily lives.

We have accepted Rotary as the vehicle before us that fulfills Your desire for us to perform charitable giving on a local and in a worldwide effort.

As Rotarians, we understand our small part in combining with others to faithfully execute our and Your duties.

We have pledged, by the Four Way Test, to "Service Above Self" with diligence and fidelity to Your Word.

Amen.

Discernment

Let us pray;
Lord, you who have given us the gifts of discernment and discretion to
conduct our Rotary and everyday lives.
Work through us to prudently discover the goodness in others and
especially goodness in our fellow Rotarians.
We pray that we may trust each others judgement as we work together to
give of our talents and treasures for the betterment of our community and
for a world living the Rotarian principals of truth, fairness, benefit and
goodwill to all concerned.
Amen.

Recollection

Let Us pray!
Dear Lord, as we gather in assembly, we pray to You to instill in us the
best of intentions in fulfilling Rotary ideals.
We have no problem in remembering the: "Four Way Test" or "Service
Above Self" when we are assembled here.
As You are aware, it sometimes becomes difficult to remember those
messages in our daily activities.
We pray that You be with us perpetually, as counsel, as we go thru
everyday life because Your principals are Rotary principals.
Amen.

2.A. IS IT THE TRUTH

Truth in Business

Let us Pray

O God of Wisdom, Light and Truth, help us to renew our dedication to truth in our

personal and business lives.

We trust your changelessness and reliability. Your truth under girds the whole universe.

O God, we honor you today by respecting truth wherever it is found; by speaking truth with integrity; and by practicing truth in all dealings.

Enrich our friendship in Rotary as we share our time together today.

Bless us as we serve.

Amen.

Friendship

Let us Pray

O God of Wisdom, Light and Truth, help us to renew our dedication to truth in our

personal and business lives.

We trust your changelessness and reliability. Your truth under girds the whole universe.

O God, we honor you today by respecting truth wherever it is found; by speaking truth with integrity; and by practicing truth in all dealings.

Enrich our friendship in Rotary as we share our time together today.

Bless us as we serve.

Amen.

Wherever Found

Let us Pray
O God of Wisdom, Light and Truth, help us to renew our dedication to truth in our personal and business lives.
We trust your changelessness and reliability. Your truth under girds the whole universe.
O God, we honor you today by respecting truth wherever it is found; by speaking truth with integrity; and by practicing truth in all dealings.
We recognize that our Rotary lives and relationships, our activities and projects are personal to us and we pray that our personalities project to those we serve.
Enrich our friendship in Rotary as we share our time together today.
Bless us as we serve.
Amen.

Recollection

Let Us Pray!
Dear Lord, as we gather in assembly, we pray to You to instill in us the best of intentions in fulfilling Rotary ideals.
We have no problem in remembering the: "Four Way Test" or "Service Above Self" when we are assembled here.
As You are aware, it sometimes becomes difficult to remember those messages in our daily activities.
We pray that You be with us perpetually, as counsel, as we go thru everyday life because Your principals are Rotary principals.
Amen.

2.B. IS IT FAIR TO ALL CONCERNED

Joy of Service

Let us Pray!
To give anonymously is the greatest satisfaction.
As You, our Lord guides us through our everyday lives, we pray to be,
meekly, last - that we may be first in Your kingdom.
By Rotarians serving others before self, we pray to maintain humility in
giving of our time, talent and treasure.
The true joy we receive - is the only reward we seek.
Lord, you who have given us the gifts of discernment and discretion to
conduct our Rotary and everyday lives.
Work through us to prudently discover the goodness in others and
especially goodness in our fellow Rotarians.
We pray that we may trust each others judgement as we work together to
give our talents and treasures for the betterment of our community and
for a world living the Rotarian principals of truth, fairness, benefit and
goodwill to all concerned.
Amen.

Give Unto Others

Let us pray,
Almighty God,
Rotarians pledge to acknowledge and question in our daily life: Is it
"Fair to all Concerned"?
Our efforts are such as to render superficial those differences that may divide us.
You, our God, have taught us to "give unto others". We do not dwell on or wonder what
others are made of. We only need to know what are their needs. Rotarians accept our
common challenges and take refuge in the good that comes to others from our efforts.
As we go thru our daily life we pledge not to define or delineate our differences, but rather
work towards common goals and "Peace Thru Service".
Inspire in us the confidence to celebrate our diversity and inclusion.
In thy name we pray,
Amen.

Relationships

Let Us Pray!
O God, who has compassion and concern for all people of every race and place, keep always before us, as Rotarians, that same loving concern.
May it infuse our relationships with each
other and with our friends and neighbors. May we extend it to all with whom we deal in daily business and social life. Whenever we sign a contract, establish a policy, or give an order, may the welfare of the other parties involved be taken into account.
O Lord, in humble recognition of your abundant goodness to us, may we never permit selfishness and greed to control our affairs.
Bless us as we gather today and may joy and peace be among us.
Amen.

A House Divided

Let us Pray!
As we come together each week we pray for your grace and guidance.
"A House Divided Cannot Stand".
Our club pledges cohesiveness and brotherhood as we dedicate ourselves to the principals of the "Four Way Test". Especially: "Is it Fair to All Concerned".
With this motto in mind, we pray to repeat it often in our actions and words in order that others see You in us and in Rotary.
Amen.

Mutual Respect

Let us Pray;
Almighty God, heavenly father, if we may humbly request, we ask You to
imbue in all Rotarians a sense of mutual respect.
May we respect all that we serve in our community and international
causes as not only those in need, but also as individuals that You have
created in Your own image. Those who have not been able to achieve as
we have, by circumstance of their environment and personal health.
We ask, also, that we achieve respect for each other as having different
gifts and motives to achieve Rotary goals. Patience and prudence with
each other, we pray, prevail in all circumstances.
We know, that by Your grace, that respect for each other will achieve the
cohesion we need to help others.
In thy name we pray.
Amen.

Religious Preferences

Let us Pray!
Almighty God, as Rotarians with Your guidance and grace, we are pledged to
understand, respect and dignify religious preferences.
As we observe dissension, Rotarians counter dissension with understanding.
As we encounter ignorance, Rotarians counter with education.
As we condemn acts of violence, Rotarians counter those acts with service.
As Rotarians extend friendship, hope and love, as You have taught us, we pray that
everyone recognize that the true value of our efforts is a world that transcends ignorance
and violence with understanding and peace.
In Thy name we pray,
Amen.

Discernment

Let us Pray;
Almighty God, you have given us the great gift of discernment. The ability to
decide for good or bad, for better or for worse or just to maintain the status quo.
As Rotarians we ask for Your counsel in all matters - that we may serve others.
As we serve, we pray to look at conditions in the eyes of the recipient and not for
our good.
As servants to mankind, in Your name, we can only retain faith in our Rotary
institution as long as we have faith in You.
Amen.

Our Blessings

Let us Pray!
Almighty God, we praise You and thank you for blessing us to live in this
sweet land of liberty and freedom to exercise our ability to choose.
With the ability You have given us to project Your will with our heart, our
mind and our intellect we pray for outcomes that will continue Your will
for us and for our individual freedom.
As we elect individuals to project Your and our will, we pray that You
bless them with the conviction and ability to defend Rotarian principals of
"Service Above Self" and "Fairness to All Concerned".
In thy name we pray,
Amen.

Equality

Let us Pray!
Almighty God, In Your eyes, all men (and women) are created equal. We are
endowed by You, our God, to promote the same kind of fairness to everyone.
Yes, we are provided by You with various abilities and talent to be used to support
and defend those less fortunate. Therefore, by combining our abilities,
It is right and just for Rotarians to accumulate knowledge of those oppressed and/or
in need and dispense our accumulated time, talent and treasure to help the welfare
and comfort for the greatest of those needs.
We pray for Your Holy Spirit to guide us to fulfill a complex mission with equality
and justice that we may satisfy Your will for us, and, to draw others to our mission.
In thy name we pray,
Amen.

The Virtues

Let Us Pray!
O Lord, in our daily application of the Four Way Test, grant us:
The virtues of patience to prudently discern others points-of-view
Temperance to thoughtfully explain our position, and
To impart justice with the fortitude Your grace gives us.
In thy grace, grant us the vision of Faith,
The inspiration of Hope, and
The blessings of Charity.
In thy name we pray!
Amen.

2.C. WILL IT BUILD GOODWILL AND BETTER FRIENDSHIPS

Integrity and Good Will

Let us Pray!
As Rotarians focus on their projects to help others throughout the world, we pray for
Your guidance that we may use the integrity and good will You have given us to cooperate
with each other to help others.
We pray our dedication and enthusiasm for Rotary prevail in this world of great need.
We pray that our energy be well guided by You, our God, to benefit mankind.
In Thy name we pray.
Amen.

Goodwill in Business

Let Us Pray!
O God, who has compassion and concern for all people of every race and place, keep
always before us, as Rotarians, that same loving concern.
May it infuse our relationships with each other and with our friends and neighbors.
May we extend it to all with whom we deal in daily business and social life. Whenever
we sign a contract, establish a policy,
or give an order, may the welfare of the other parties involved be taken into account.
O Lord, in humble recognition of your abundant goodness to us, may we never
permit selfishness and greed to
control our affairs.
Bless us as we gather today and may joy and peace be among us in our everyday
business.
In thy name we pray,
Amen.

Discernment and Discretion

Let us Pray!
Lord, you who have given us the gifts of discernment and discretion to conduct our Rotary and everyday lives.
Work through us to prudently discover the goodness in others and especially goodness in our fellow Rotarians.
We pray that we may trust each others judgement as we work together to give of our talents and treasures for the betterment of our community and for a world of Rotarian principals.
Amen.

Visiting Rotarians

Let us Pray!
Almighty God, we thank You and praise You for blessing us with Rotarian visitors to our club.
As they add to our fellowship and energy we can only thank You for their giving attitude to enhance a common belief in Rotary principals.
We pray that as they leave us, that they travel in safety and bring back to their home clubs a sense of who we all are as Rotarians.
In thy name we pray.
Amen.

Projects

Let us Pray!

As Rotarians focus on their projects to help others throughout the world, we pray for Your guidance that we may use the integrity and good will You have given us to cooperate with each other to help others.

We pray our dedication and enthusiasm for Rotary prevail in this world of great need.

We pray that our energy be well guided by You, our God, to benefit mankind.

In Thy name we pray.

Amen

Bridging Cultures

Let us Pray!

Almighty God, as Rotarians take action locally and globally each day, we ask Your guidance for our members as we pour our passion, integrity, and intelligence into completing projects that have a lasting impact.

We pray to persevere until we deliver real, lasting solutions as we bridge cultures and connect continents to champion peace, fight illiteracy and poverty, promote clean water and sanitation, and fight disease.

In Thy name we pray,

Amen.

Fortitude

Almighty God,

Recent events, which we judge to be both unjustified and unpunished, cannot perpetuate if our Republic is to continue and thrive on the basis of "Liberty and Justice for all".

We pray, O Lord, for the resolve to defend America against its dissolution.

We ask for Your intercession in the affairs of all by re-inforcing our hearts with the fortitude and will desired by our mutual love for each other.

We pray that as Rotarians practice the building of good will, that we build a contagion of better friendships to heal the destructive practices we see.

We pray for Your grace that our link is the good we do, to create an infectious chain of good that overcomes the evil we see.

In thy name we pray,

Amen.

2.D. WILL IT BE BENEFICIAL TO ALL CONCERNED

Fairness

Let us Pray!

Almighty God, In Your eyes, all men (and women) are created equal. We are endowed by You, our God, to promote the same kind of fairness to everyone.

Yes, we are provided by You with various abilities and talent to be used to support and defend those less fortunate. Therefore, by combining our abilities,

It is right and just for Rotarians to accumulate knowledge of those oppressed and/or in need and dispense our accumulated time, talent and treasure to help the welfare and comfort for the greatest of those needs.

We pray for Your Holy Spirit to guide us to fulfill a complex mission with equality and justice that we may satisfy Your will for us, and, to draw others to our mission.

In thy name we pray,

Amen.

Youth Exchange

Let us Pray!

Almighty God, we appreciate the insight that Rotary has given us to work with the exchange of youth, with their fresh thinking and open mind.

We enjoy the opportunity to understand future cooperation and development, and invest in the interest of those we previously knew little about.

As we wash away prejudice for other cultures and encourage unity of heart and mind, we pray for Your continued guidance as new ideas from those we may have held previous differences, are revealed.

In thy name we pray.

Amen!

Lasting Change

Let us pray;
Almighty God, as Rotarians You have challenged us to act together and see a world where
people unite and take action to create lasting improvement in the lives of others.
Across the globe: in our communities, and in ourselves, our neighbors and our friends, we
ask for Your guidance to take action to create lasting change that is
"Beneficial to all concerned."
We ask that by Your Grace, that we pour our passion, integrity, and intelligence into
completing projects that have a lasting impact.
We pray to remember Rotary history, for more than 110 years, Rotarians have bridged
cultures and connected continents to champion peace, fight illiteracy and poverty,
promote clean water and sanitation, and fight disease.
May we persevere until we deliver real, lasting solutions to create lasting change.
We pray for Your continued grace!
Amen.

Rotary Areas of Focus

Let us Pray!
Almighty God, as Rotarians take action locally and globally each day, we
ask Your guidance for our members as we pour our passion, integrity, and
intelligence into completing projects that have a lasting impact.
We pray to persevere until we deliver real, lasting solutions as we bridge
cultures and connect continents to champion peace, fight illiteracy and
poverty, promote clean water and sanitation, and fight disease.
In Thy name we pray,
Amen.

Areas of Focus

Let us pray;

Almighty God, our hope is in you.

We pray for the inspiration and tenacity to perform our Rotary mission.

At a time when worldwide confusion and change envelope our thinking, we pray You guide us out of the malaise that inevitably sets in to our thinking and performance.

Rotarians are practiced and aware of the needs of others.

We pray that counting on each other becomes the impetus and inspiration to bring us to greater levels of dedication working with each other.

As we take the necessary steps toward success in Rotary's areas of focus, we pray our planning and cooperation with all Rotarians bring all the dynamics to change the world.

In thy name we pray,

Amen

Diversity

Let us pray,

Almighty God, we pray that you protect and encourage the Rotary global network as we strive to build a world where people unite and take action to create lasting change.

As Rotary values diversity and celebrates the contributions of people of all backgrounds, we pray for Rotary to grow and diversify our membership to make sure we reflect the communities we serve.

As we create an organization that is more open and inclusive, fair to all, builds goodwill, and benefits our communities we pray for people with differing perspectives and ideas who will help Rotary take action.

In thy name we pray,

Amen

Peace thru Service

Let us pray,

Almighty God,

Rotarians pledge to acknowledge and question in our daily life: Is it

"Fair to all Concerned"?

Our efforts are such as to render superficial those differences that may divide us.

You, our God, have taught us to "give unto others". We do not dwell on or wonder what

others are made of. We only need to know what are their needs. Rotarians accept our

common challenges and take refuge in the good that comes to others from our efforts.

As we go thru our daily life we pledge not to define or delineate our differences, but rather

work towards common goals and "Peace Thru Service".

Inspire in us the confidence to celebrate our diversity and inclusion.

In thy name we pray,

Amen.

3. ROTARY CORE PRINCIPALS

Going Beyond —-

Let us Pray;
As Rotarians we follow Your call, Almighty God, to go beyond "doing
unto others as we would have done to us".
By adopting the motto: "Service Above Self" Rotarians are committed to
go beyond caring, or concern or empathy.
With compassion for others less fortunate we pray for Your Grace and
Guidance by performing.
Performing to provide services for: Peace and Conflict Resolution, Health
and Disease Prevention, Clean Water and Education among other core
programs to create lasting change.
"Service above Self" for Rotarians means compassion and performance
for others.
In thy name we pray,
Amen.

The Challenge

Let us Pray!
Almighty God, as Rotarians You have challenged us to act together and see a world where
people unite and take action to create last improvement in the lives of others.
Across the globe: in our communities, and in ourselves, our neighbors and our friends, we
ask for Your guidance to take action to create lasting change.
ideas, join leaders, and take action.
We ask that by Your Grace, that we pour our passion, integrity, and intelligence into
completing projects that have a lasting impact.
May we persevere until we deliver real, lasting solutions to create lasting change.
We pray to remember Rotary history, for more than 110 years, Rotarians have bridged
cultures and connected continents to champion peace, fight illiteracy and poverty,
promote clean water and sanitation, and fight disease.
We pray for Your continued grace!
Amen.

4. EIGHT AREAS OF ROTARY FOCUS

Hope

Let us pray,

Almighty God, as Hope is a Rotarian motivator: we give this gift to others
thru the divine inspiration you give us.

That inspiration has to be given to others, our clients, our brethren, thru
the deeds we perform.

Give hope to those that need clean water, need health and care to live a life
of security but allow for a way out of a world of poverty. To be able to raise
their families as a quest in loving you, our God, knowing that ultimately

You will provide

In thy name we pray,

Amen.

4A. POLIO PLUS

Foundation Support

POLIO PLUS

Let us Pray;
This month, our Rotary Foundation asks us to consider the Area of Focus: Disease Prevention and Treatment. Our principal effort is for Polio eradication and we pray for your grace for this and all Rotary efforts in Disease Prevention and Treatment.
We are indeed close to global eradication and cannot give up while on the edge of success. The support we are now getting from local authorities and tribes in the remaining endemic areas is heartening, and by Your grace we pray to You for success.
Our strength comes from You and our global partners.
Rotarians also support health initiative all over the world wherever there are under-served. Rural health clinics receive the time, talent and treasure of Rotarians. Our clubs support dental clinics, eye clinics, wellness baby screenings and multiple varieties of other initiatives in third world countries and right here in our own communities.
We will continue to pray for Your grace that we may provide helpful services for those in need.
In thy name we pray,
Amen.

Vast Rotary Sea

Let us Pray;
Almighty God, as a small island in a vast Rotary sea, we ask for your guidance as we assemble to deliberate the depth of our commitment.
The tide of Rotary values, as we fulfill them, cover the earth with the best of what You have given us.
That tide is conquering Polio, educating those otherwise lost in poverty, feeding the hungry, and giving drink to the thirsty.
We ask You, our God, that our club pride, in combination with others, propels us into a future where all our efforts result in oceans of hope and belief in You - who alone brings peace and joy in Your worldly kingdom.
Amen.

Inoculation

Let is Pray;
A major area of focus for us, as Rotarians, is Disease Prevention and Treatment.
As daunting as this goal may be, we ask You to bless us in our efforts to do all that
we, a small group of participants, can dedicate ourselves to.
We pray that those areas of the world that are closed off to inoculation and
education will respond to Your will and submit to our help.
As we make progress in Your name please help all Rotarians to persevere in our
quest to improve others health.
In thy name we pray,
Amen.

Focus

Let us Pray!
As Rotarians focus on their projects to help others throughout the world, we pray
for Your guidance that we may use the integrity and good will You have given us
to cooperate with each other to help others.
We pray our dedication and enthusiasm for Rotary prevail in this world of
continued great need for the eradication of Polio.
We pray that our energy be well guided by You, our God, to benefit mankind.
In Thy name we pray.
Amen.

Giving of Ourselves

Let us pray!

We, as Rotarians, are asked to share our time, our talent, and our treasure as the fruits of a lifetime of hard work with those that are not as fortunate as ourselves. As we generously and selectively do our best to fulfill the humanitarian goals You have given us, we pray for Your guidance in making the right decisions that provide maximum benefit for those that need help.

For the greater love we are compelled to give in thy name, may we be consoled by the unity Rotarians have and the knowledge that You are with us.

In thy name we pray.

Amen.

4B. CLEAN WATER AND SANITATION

Health and Water

Let Us Pray!
Almighty God, as we work for Rotary's goal of Peace and Conflict
Resolution, we pray not to lose sight of those components under the
control You have given us.
We pray that our educational programs be always in your sight that by
Your reason we may influence those in our care and guidance to be good
citizens of our community, their country and Your world.
By Rotary Health and Water programs we pray that successes are fruitful
in removing nation and personal barriers in the underdeveloped world for
the greater security of all.
In Thy name we pray!
Amen.

Dignity

Let Us Pray!
We pray for life: peace and dignity by our service for You.
We embrace Your idea that all human life should be respected, dignified and
protected. Rotary principals and your principals to dignify human life by its
preservation thru our acts of kindness and charity.
We pray our actions to help our fellow citizens in your name give us the
enthusiasm to present Rotary programs to ensure development with clean water,
food and basic human needs.
We understand that you are in charge of the beginnings of life and that we can
only work for your ideals in life's development after birth.
May our minor efforts find favor with You in providing for others needs.
In thy name we pray,
Amen.

Productivity thru Health

Let us pray,

Almighty God, we pray for continued Rotary success for clean water, sanitation, and hygiene education as basic necessities for a healthy environment and a productive life. We understand that when people have access to clean water and sanitation, waterborne diseases decrease, children stay healthier and attend school more regularly, and mothers can spend less time carrying water and more time helping their families.

We pray for Your inspiration and grace to help Rotarians mobilize resources, form partnerships, and invest in infrastructure and training that yield long-term change for clean water and sanitation.

In thy name we pray,

Amen.

Water and Sanitation

Let us pray!

Almighty God, as we reflect on the precious gifts you have given us with our children and grand children, we pray for your guidance to Rotarians to help and protect the mothers and children of those less fortunate than ourselves

We pray for mankind to secure adequate water, food and sanitation for their well being.

We embrace this core necessity of people throughout the world.

May we be all aware of starvation and thirst in undeveloped areas in Africa and Haiti - as our own neighbors.

We pray that efforts of rotarians to alleviate their hunger may be successful.

We conceive and believe that, with Your help, world peace can be achieved by our effors.

In thy name we pray,

Amen.

Water, Food and Sanitation

Let us pray!

Almighty God, we pray for mankind to secure adequate water, food and sewerage for their well being. As Rotarians, we embrace this core necessity of people throughout the world.

May we be all aware of starvation and thirst in underdeveloped areas in Africa and Haiti - as our own neighbor.

We pray that efforts of rotarians to alleviate their hunger may be successful.

We conceive and believe that, with Your help, world peace can be achieved by our efforts.

Amen

4C. HEALTH AND DISEASE PREVENTION

Dedication Month

Let us pray!

Almighty God, this month, our Rotary Foundation asks us to consider the Area of Focus: Disease Prevention and Treatment. We aren't just about Polio Eradication, although that has been a huge campaign for several decades.

We are indeed close to global eradication and cannot give up while on the edge of success. Remembering there have been *(consult rotary.org for current numbers)* and we are days away from this year's end. The support we are now getting from local authorities and tribes in the remaining endemic areas is heartening. Our global partners are not giving up and neither will we.

Rotarians also support health initiative all over the world wherever there are underserved. Rural health clinics receive the time, talent and treasure of Rotarians. Our clubs support dental clinics, eye clinics, baby screenings and multiple varieties of other initiatives in third world countries and right here in our own communities.

We ask for Your guidance and confidence that Rotarians perform this mission.

In thy name we pray,

Amen.

Disease Prevention

Let us pray:

Almighty God, we pray for your guidance this month, as our Rotary Foundation asks us to consider the Rotary Area of Focus: Disease Prevention and Treatment.

We aren't just about Polio Eradication, although that has been a huge campaign for several decades. We are indeed close to global eradication and cannot give up while on the edge of success. Remember there have been only 31 cases in 2016 and we are days away from this year's end.

The support we are now getting from local authorities and tribes in the remaining endemic areas is heartening. Our global partners are not giving up and neither will we.

Rotarians also support health initiative all over the world wherever there are underserved. Rural health clinics receive the time, talent and treasure of Rotarians. Our clubs support dental clinics, eye clinics, well baby screenings and multiple varieties of other initiatives in third world countries and right here in our own communities.

We pray for Your continued grace in Rotary initiatives,

Amen.

Inoculation

Let is Pray;
A major area of focus for us, as Rotarians, is Disease Prevention and Treatment. As daunting as this goal may be, we ask You to bless us in our efforts to do all that we, a small group of participants, can dedicate ourselves to.
We pray that those areas of the world that are closed off to inoculation and education will respond to Your will and submit to our help. As we make progress in Your name please help all Rotarians to persevere in our quest to improve others health.
In thy name we pray,
Amen.

Be Not Afraid

Let us pray;
Almighty God, our hope is in you.
We take to heart your abundant grace and invocation to"Be not afraid".
In our time of crisis, in this period of our isolation from one another, we pray to continue our Rotary mission of improving health and disease prevention in a troubled world.
We pray for those in need of the hope that You provide. Take those who succumb to disease into Your heavenly home.
May those that become infected be imbued with the hope and optimism that faith in You provide for their healing.
For caregivers, who selflessly put themselves in harms way, we pray that You help them maintain their sense of mission with dedication and enthusiasm because they have the ability to inspire all.
As we take measures to meet our mission, we pray to use collective Rotary minds and intellect to find ways to communicate mission as a great challenge.
In this time of crisis we pray for the enthusiasm to stick to our cause.
As your humble servants, we understand that communication through our prayer to You is the greatest communication.
In thy name we pray,
Amen.

Children's Health

Let us pray!
Almighty God, heavenly father we are obliged as Rotarians and as Your
children to engage and assist those that are less fortunate than ourselves.
Especially our children.
Rotarians are committed to helping children and families worldwide by
eliminating the burden of disease and deformities in order to give them a
life of joy and fulfillment.
We pray that You guide us in helping those that program assistance and
care - to give all a fair chance at the life You have planned for us.
With the complications of facilitating missions, counseling, collaboration,
and education - the mission is daunting. With Your counseling and grace
we pray that all may be healed to live productive lives.
In Thy name we pray,
Amen.

Children's Health

Let us Pray;
Almighty God, we thank You and pray to You for the health
and safety of our children.
As Rotarians continue to give to causes to improve the lives of those
generations following, we ask for Your blessing on their efforts for self
development. We also ask that You continue to protect them in
development of a health body, mind and spirit.
Rotarians continue to provide scholarships for their education. Rotarians
seek to improve children's health by eliminating disease and create good
health habits. We turn to You to instill in our children the spirit to develop
Rotarian values and then pass on this Your will, for all.
Our cause is Your cause. Give us the will to sacrifice what is necessary in
the development of future generations.
In thy name we pray,
Amen.

Freedom of Movement

Let us pray,
Almighty God, as You bless America with Your unbounded grace, we pray all to take the renewed freedom we are experiencing seriously. Rotarians understand that we are blessed to share our gifts with gratitude and a spirit of respect for others health and well being.
As we gradually progress to total freedom of movement and affiliation with others, we ask to never forget the tragedy that many others have endured during the worst of times.
As professionals work to provide cures for illness, we pray all to understand these difficult times as prologue to a world of peace and dedication to improved health and wellness.
In thy name we pray,
Amen.

Distance Between Rotarians

Let us pray;
Almighty God, as we experience distance between us and our fellow Rotarians we rely on You to give us the strength to carry forward our goals for our family, friends and for Rotary.
In all trying times, our respect for each other lets us use the guidelines You have given us to provide "Service above Self".
Respect is critical to our fight. It is essential to turning the tide against our common health enemy. There is no path out of this test of Rotary dedication and will on our own. Without Your guidance our efforts cannot succeed.
By Your grace we pray You protect those that, by their choice, are engaged in nursing our way ahead in gratitude.
In thy name we pray,
Amen.

Priorities

Let Us Pray!
We are pleased to be motivated by You to work toward Rotary principals.
We pray that our time, our health and the health of our loved ones, will allow us
to be good Rotarians in terms of service, to our club and the community.
For those who receive our service, we wish Your continued presence in their lives
for their support and comfort.
We pray that our priorities recognize Rotary as part of who we are with our time,
our treasure and talent.
Amen.

Prevention

Let is Pray;
As Rotarians focus on Disease Prevention and Treatment, we pray for
Your guidance of our local providers.
Please guide them in their education, analysis and treatment of those in
our community who need their skills, dedication and care.
As we make progress in Your name, please help all Rotarians to persevere
in our quest to improve others health.
In thy name we pray,
Amen!

Drug Use

Let us Pray!
Almighty God, heavenly father we ask for Your consolation and grace that we understand and implement programs to relieve the pain that others may experience.
We understand that their pain is sometimes alleviated by medical and drug treatment. We pray to be part of the education of our family and community in council to understand others symptoms and to help them to reduce their need for overusing medications.
We pray that You will guide Rotarians to educate and encourage youth not to indulge in the destructive use of drugs by implementing Rotary Youth leadership, mentoring and exchange programs.
In Thy name we pray! Amen.

Thy Will

Let us pray,
Almighty God,
You have endowed us with the consciousness and the ability, to overcome the problems we see before us.
With this individual gift of Your grace, we pray You empower Rotarians with the motivation to fulfill Your will and apply our mind, our intellect and our will to the surmountable obstacles that become ever-present in our focus.
We have no power except the good judgement You have given us. Rotarians accept Your gift and find resolution to greater successes with Your will and the ability You have given us.
During this time of great anxiety for the health of others give us the strength and ability to overcome this time of great suffering, fear and great mourning. We pray that the current pain inflicted on mankind be transformed by You and lead to a new springtime of hope and devotion with the Rotary power of a unified spirit.
In thy name we pray,
Amen.

Rotarian Communion

Let us pray,
Almighty God, Heavenly Father
we pray as we maintain communion with each other in common cause and take
inspiration from our motto: "Service Above Self".
As our Communion of Rotary like minds and spirit are being tested, as are all those
subject to severe health concerns, we take solace knowing
You have given us the ability to adapt creatively to socially distance ourselves from each
other. We know that You are with us in communion without distance.
As we endeavor to embrace all those with health hardships and, as we make the best of the
Burden of Separation from each other, we reflect on not being separated from You. We
gather inspiration and hope
as we muster Rotarian talents and abilities to persevere under difficult circumstances. Our
hope in communion with You can only make Rotarians stronger in our dedication for
"Peace thru Service".
In thy name we pray,
Amen.

Human Spirit

Let us Pray;
Almighty God,
We are thankful that You have given us the 7 great attributes of the human spirit:
First, Our Body: as a tabernacle of Your design to nourish and maintain
at maximum health.
Our heart: the center of our being distributing more than life giving fluid and
nourishment, but containing our faith and trust in You to absorb and feel
regeneration of Your will for us.
Our mind: that dwells on the importance of giving of ourselves to others
Our memory: of the vast amalgam of learning and experience of so many that
have done Your work through Rotary
Our intellect: to clarify. When combined with other Rotarians we dynamically produce
projects that are good, true and beautiful for a better world.
Our will: and desire to enthusiastically generate unselfish improvements
to the social order.
And finally: our soul which reflects who we are and how we are recognized as Rotarians.
In thy name we pray,
Amen.

Difficult Year

Let us pray,
Almighty God, we praise you and thank you for bringing us thru a
difficult year of health concerns for rotarians and their families.
You have blessed us as we live in a place of relative calm in a sea of
anxiety. Our thoughts and prayers to You are for the continued safety and
health of Rotarians, family and friends who are less fortunate.
As we enter a new calendar year we ask for Your continued guidance. We
pray that we may project Your compassion and will as Rotary projects
continue this new year.
In thy name we pray,
Amen.

Care Givers

Let us Pray!
Almighty God, heavenly father we pray for those that protect us and serve
to make sure that societies order and peace is preserved.
We are thankful for the extreme dedication they possess with the
motivation to train constantly that we may enjoy the American way of life
in peace and security.
We pray for their safety as they go into harms way to assure our safety,
and that we, as Rotarians and citizens, find the courage to perform with
fidelity as their guidance requires.
Be with them, O Lord, knowing that we, those that they serve, are thankful
for their dedication to us and to their families.
Amen.

Health
Cardinal Virtues

Let Us Pray!

As Rotarians, we are thankful for the gifts you have given us for
ourselves and our families that we may pass on to those in need:

The gift of the memory of those that have gone before us,

The gift of health and the energy and heart to help others,

The gift of intellect and knowledge thru education and experience,

The gift of will and the drive to persist in our efforts,

The gift of discernment that we may prioritize our efforts, and

The gift of the soul given us in Your word.

Amen.

Cognitive Impairment

Let us Pray!

We pray for those in our midst that may be degenerating in mind and body.

We pray that they may be at peace with You and the world around them.

We recognize that our thoughtfulness and attention to others is a cornerstone of Rotary.

We ask You to keep us ever mindful of their contribution to our families and to society.

May we recognize always their experience and attention to us and others in their long
and productive lives, and pray that their spirit
be passed on to us by Your grace.

Amen

Decline

Let us Pray!
Almighty God and father of all, as Rotarians we continue to
experience the decline of our loved ones.
We do pray for their recovery and realize their slow departure
from us and their welcome by You.
We pray for those that see to their welfare and show with
loving care respect as they share in their memories together.
As a family of Rotarians, we pray to share with the caregivers
among us their loving experience.
In Thy name we pray,
Amen.

Fundraising

Let Us Pray!
We are motivated to be Rotarians and work towards Rotary principals.
Since we are also motivated by Your will, we pray that our Rotary
efforts can fulfill our deepest longing to please You.
We know that each Rotary project, each fundraising is difficult to fully
complete by most of us.
We pray that our time, our health and the health of our loved ones,
will allow us the motivation to be good Rotarians, in terms of service,
to our club and the community.
We pray that our priorities recognize Rotary as part of who we are
with our time, our treasure and talent.
Amen.

Freedom

Let us pray,
Almighty God, as You bless America with Your unbounded grace, we
pray all to take the renewed freedom we are experiencing seriously.
Rotarians understand that we are blessed to share our gifts with gratitude
and a spirit of respect for others health and well being.
As we gradually progress to total freedom of movement and affiliation
with others, we ask to never forget the tragedy that many others have
endured during the worst of times.
As professionals work to provide cures for illness, we pray all to
understand these difficult times as prologue to a world of peace and
dedication to improved health and wellness.
In thy name we pray,
Amen.

Overcoming Distance

Let us pray;
Almighty God, as we experience distance between us and our fellow
Rotarians we rely on You to give us the strength to carry forward our goals
for our family, friends and for Rotary.
In all trying times, our respect for each other lets us use the guidelines You
have given us to provide "Service above Self".
Respect is critical to our fight. It is essential to turning the tide against our
common health enemy. There is no path out of this test of Rotary
dedication and will on our own. Without Your guidance our efforts
cannot succeed.
By Your grace we pray You protect those that, by their choice, are engaged
in nursing our way ahead in gratitude.
In thy name we pray,
Amen.

Inoculation

Let is Pray;
A major area of focus for us, as Rotarians, is Disease Prevention and Treatment.
As daunting as this goal may be, we ask You to bless us in our efforts to do all that
we, a small group of participants, can dedicate ourselves to.
We pray that those areas of the world that are closed off to inoculation and
education will respond to Your will and submit to our help.
As we make progress in Your name please help all Rotarians to persevere in our
quest to improve others health.
In thy name we pray,
Amen.

Fortitude

Let us Pray;
If not for You, Almighty God, mankind could not have progressed in
goodness and service to our fellows. Remembering this long and
successful road to wellness, Rotarians and those that serve require the
quality of fortitude You give us.
As we, together with Your grace, have successfully developed answers to
pressing problems, we pray for Your guidance in the eradication of disease
and the concurrent tragedy of the loss of hope we all now face.
Please be with those that suffer and offer them the strength to persevere
through their affliction and pain.
As we pray for those in jeopardy of disease, may we, as Rotarians retain
the spirit to "answer the call" to help.
In thy name we pray,
Amen.

With a Suffering Spirit

Let us Pray:

As children of God and Rotarians we are well aware and thankful for our
health and well being as we enjoy this beautiful place.

We are aware that some of us, and those close to us, do suffer from ailments
and deteriorating health.

We pray that your Spirit will encircle them and provide them with the
comfort they need.

Help them to realize, as well, that their club is with them in their time of trial.

Amen.

Prayer for Missing Rotarians

Let us Pray!

We pray, o Lord, for Your continued consideration of those members of
our Rotary Club that cannot be with us for health reasons;

Roy Birkland for the care of his wife Pat.

Ralph Lalli for the care of his wife Lorraine.

Pam Michel and Dottie Weiner.

As loyal Rotarians they have given of themselves for many years and we
pray that we may be ever mindful of that commitment.

As we progress together with You in Your work, O Lord, we pray that You
continue to guide us all in our efforts and in the care of our families.

Amen.

Use of Time, Talent and Treasure

Let Us Pray!
We are pleased to be motivated by You to work toward Rotary principals.
We pray that our time, our health and the health of our loved ones, will allow
us to be good Rotarians, in terms of service, to our club and the community.
For those who receive our service, we wish Your continued presence in their
lives for their support and comfort.
We pray that our priorities recognize Rotary as part of who we are with our
time, our treasure and talent.
Amen.

Comfort

Let us Pray:
As children of God and Rotarians we are well aware and thankful for our
health and well being as we enjoy this beautiful place.
We are aware that some of us, and those close to us, do suffer from ailments
and deteriorating health.
We pray that your Spirit will encircle them and provide them with the
comfort they need.
Help them to realize, as well, that their club is with them in their time of trial.
Amen.

Cancer

Let us Pray!

Almighty God

We praise you and thank you for preserving the health of those here present and pray that you attend to the health of those we hold dear to us.

All of us have been touched in some way by the scourge of Cancer and understand the scourging of your Son, Jesus and the profound nature of His suffering.

We, with Your help, have achieved some measure of success preserving the lives of those afflicted with this dreaded evil.

We take courage from examples of those who have survived and ask for your guidance to all that are involved in research and care of Cancer victims.

Thru thy name we pray.

Amen

Self Health

Let us Pray!

O God, we are in awe of Your insight and guidance as Rotarians. We are obliged to be aware of our own health and personal well being as much as we are concerned with others welfare.

We understand that without our own ability to perform the tasks that are before us, we cannot fulfill Your will and be of benefit to others and their needs.

We thank You for the talents and expertise of all who administer to us and to all those that we cherish, in order that we may perform Your service to others.

In thy name we pray,

Amen.

Local Providers

Let is Pray;
As Rotarians focus on Disease Prevention and Treatment, we pray for
Your guidance of our local providers.
Please guide them in their education, analysis and treatment of those in
our community who need their skills, dedication and care.
As we make progress in Your name, please help all Rotarians to persevere
in our quest to improve others health.
In thy name we pray,
Amen!

Priorities

Let Us Pray!
We are motivated to be Rotarians and work towards Rotary
principals.
Since we are also motivated by Your will, we pray that our Rotary
efforts can fulfill our deepest longing to please You.

We know that each Rotary project, each fundraising is difficult to
fully complete by most of us.

We pray that our time, our health and the health of our loved
ones, will allow us the motivation to be good Rotarians, in terms of
service, to our club and the community.

We pray that our priorities recognize Rotary as part of who we are
with our time, our treasure and talent.
Amen.

Healing

Let us pray!
Almighty God, heavenly father we are obliged as Rotarians and as Your
children to engage and assist those that are less fortunate than ourselves.
Especially our children.
Rotarians are committed to helping children and families worldwide by
eliminating the burden of disease and deformities in order to give them a
life of joy and fulfillment.
We pray that You guide us in helping those that program assistance and
care - to give all a fair chance at the life You have planned for us.
With the complications of facilitating missions, counseling, collaboration,
and education - the mission is daunting. With Your counseling and grace
we pray that all may be healed to live productive lives.
In Thy name we pray,
Amen.

Children

Let us Pray;
Almighty God, we thank You and pray to You for the health and safety of our children.
As Rotarians continue to give to causes to improve the lives of those generations
following, we ask for Your blessing on their efforts for self development. We also ask that
You continue to protect them in development of a health body, mind and spirit.
Rotarians continue to provide scholarships for their education. Rotarians seek to improve
children's health by eliminating disease and create good health habits. We turn to You to
instill in our children the spirit to develop Rotarian values and then pass on this
Your will, for all.
Our cause is Your cause. Give us the will to sacrifice what is necessary in
the development of future generations.
In thy name we pray,
Amen.

Fundraising

Let Us Pray!
We are motivated to be Rotarians and work towards Rotary principals.
Since we are also motivated by Your will, we pray that our Rotary efforts
can fulfill our deepest longing to please You.
We know that each Rotary project, each fundraising is difficult to fully
complete by most of us.
We pray that our time, our health and the health of our loved ones, will
allow us the motivation to be good Rotarians, in terms of service, to our
club and the community.
We pray that our priorities recognize Rotary as part of who we are with
our time, our treasure and talent.
Amen.

Health and Welfare

Let us pray!
Almighty God, heavenly father we pray for the health and welfare of our children.
We pray that all parents take the responsibility and be inspired with the love and faith
You have given us to dedicate to future generations.
We pray that caregivers, teachers and child advocates nurture and protect
those in their care.
We pray that children may develop childhood memories making them good citizens and,
as Your children, that they project that image to future generations.
In thy name we pray!
Amen.

In Rotary Service

Let us pray;
Almighty God, as we come together today to contemplate our personal
well being, we pray to You to help us understand and dedicate our
health efforts as protecting the life You have given us.
We understand that when we are in good health we are better able to serve
You as Rotarians.
We pray for strength in our bodies, our hearts and our minds: that our
memory, our intellect and our souls may act in purity and dedication to
the love of others.
In this coming year we pray that Rotary success is a reflection of all that
You have given us.
In thy name we pray,
Amen.

Hero's Song

Let us pray;
Songs are sung of hero's past, of those distinguished in battle, or elevated
to great position.
But what of the great mass of mankind who, by God's grace, performed with
valor, honor and without the glory of worldly recognition.
Those that did what had to be done in their time and in a way that gives glory to
God: unselfish and tempered by their time. Those unsung.
They live today, in a different way, a different place, as warriors in public service
and are spontaneous in doing right in a time of crisis.
They have learned to do right sometimes by how they were brought up and then
through training. They live among us.
Respect and honor. Unselfish. Hero's are not to be worshiped, they do not care to
be worshiped. If ego exists in the hero, question whether they are hero's?
Duty, honor, country, community.
The live where dedication to duty is distinctive and valor is common.
Where their working realm is a zone apart, not to be pierced by outside thought.
The hero mocks the self proclaimed by his humility, his simple act of not reacting
in his own self interest. He does not proclaim he is the greatest, the best. Those
that are self adorned.
His cause is not himself.
The hero does and walks away. He hides in the comfort of duty performed.
In thy name we pray,
Amen.

4D. FIGHTING ILLITERACY AND POVERTY

Health

Let us pray!
Almighty God, heavenly father we are obliged as Rotarians and as Your children to
engage and assist those that are less fortunate than ourselves. Especially our children.
Rotarians are committed to helping children and families worldwide by eliminating the
burden of disease and deformities in order to give them a life of joy and fulfillment.
We pray that You guide us in helping those that program assistance and care - to give all a
fair chance at the life You have planned for us.
With the complications of facilitating missions, counseling, collaboration, and education
- the mission is daunting. With Your counseling and grace we pray that all may be healed
to live productive lives.
In Thy name we pray,
Amen.

Scholarship Committee

Let us Pray
Almighty God, we thank you and praise You for overlooking our projects and
fundraising. Our efforts would not be successful without the grace You provide.
We pray that You oversee our Scholarship Committee that they be ever mindful of your
guidance in the challenge of providing funds for the most needy and worthy of applicants.
We pray that those we try to help may be blessed to make progress in their lives and give
back to others as we have tried to give to them.
May the spirit of Rotary be Your spirit and inspire by You all others we come
in contact with.
In Thy name we pray.
Amen.

Scholarship

Let us Pray;
Lord we pray that our small part be blessed by Your Holy Spirit as we select
worthy students for help in furthering their education.
All those here understand that we must do Your work with others and guide
them towards their goals as they pursue their own value in a world much in
need of souls that can be educated to the greater good of their fellows.
We pray that our tradition of giving to others can be transplanted to them by
our own work.
With Your inspiration.
Amen.

The Future

Let Us Pray!
We, as Rotarians, recognize that our Students are the future. The future of our country
and of our world. The future of our families and of Rotary.
In your infinite wisdom Lord, You have given Rotarians the ability to choose what is right
and true from all the choices we have.
As Rotary is able to continue because of Your right principles, we pray that we may carry
on Your will thru those that will succeed us.
We pray that our students recognize that Rotary principals are Your principles and bring
those principles with them into the future.
Amen.

Service Above Self

Let Us Pray!
We pray for the Holy Spirit to be with those that are entrusted with our
precious students.
May they be inspired with the dedication necessary for no greater calling
than to pass on knowledge and experience.
As Rotarians, we pray that our teachers provide our students to be well
rounded in thought, actions and willingness to give back to others and to
pass on "Service Above Self" to succeeding generations.
Amen.

Core Value

Let us pray;
Almighty God, we pray to You for guidance as Rotarians as we support education and the
work of our educators in our community.
As education, as a core Rotary value, we share in the great joy in seeing our students
develop as citizens and those dedicated to the values You have described for us as adults.
We understand, that the efforts we enjoy providing to our students, are in small measure
only a beginning, and pray that You inspire our students with the grace and joy to use the
abilities You have given them for their good and for those that follow.
Amen.

Freedom to Learn

Let us Pray;
Almighty God, we pray for all to have the Freedom to learn. With Your grace, we pray
that we, as Rotarians, will continue to promote education throughout the world.
With freedom, may we promote and encourage all to learn with Rotary's core belief in:
college scholarships and Peace Fellowships, thru RYLA, Global Exchange, formation for
tomorrows leaders and Interact.
As global citizens uniting for the common good, we know that with Your grace we can
accomplish even more.
Amen.

Good Counsel

Let us Pray;
Almighty God, heavenly father of good council,
You, who came as a teacher for all mankind and revealed that true teaching is
from the will of God.
We praise You and thank You for the education we and our families have received
and, as Rotarians, pledge Rotary's core Area of Focus for Basic Education and
Literacy for everyone to promote Peace and Conflict Resolution.
We ask You to bless our own Good Will thru education: RYLA, Youth Exchange,
S4TL, Interact, the Dictionary Program and our Scholarship Program.
Give us the wisdom to discern and to promote these programs as we demonstrate
Your teaching to us.
Amen.

Literacy

Let us pray!

Almighty God, we pray to You for guidance as Rotarians as we support Basic Education and Literacy and the work of our educators in our community.

As education, as a core Rotary value and area of focus, we share in the great joy in seeing our students develop as citizens and those dedicated to the values You have described for us as adults.

We understand, that the efforts we enjoy providing to our students, are in small measure only a beginning, and pray that You inspire our students with the grace and joy to use the abilities You have given them for their good and for those that follow.

Amen.

Gift of Generations

Let Us Pray!

Almighty God, we are thankful for the gift of generations.

As Rotarians, we accept our responsibility to instruct and inform those succeeding us by right ethical and moral conduct in all that they do.

Our classroom is the example we set in "Service Above Self" and participation in educational programs in our community.

We pray that our experience in all things be measured by our faith in You, our God and those that you have endowed to instruct generations to follow.

Amen.

Educators

Let us pray;
Almighty God,
we pray to You for guidance as Rotarians as we support education and the work of our
educators in our community.
As education, a core Rotary value, we share in the great joy in seeing our students develop
as citizens and those dedicated to the values You have proscribed for us as adults.
We understand, that the efforts we enjoy providing to our students, are in small measure
only a beginning, and pray that You inspire our students with the grace and joy to use the
abilities You have given them for their good and for those that follow.
Amen.

Nurture and Protect

Let us pray!
Almighty God,
We pray that caregivers, teachers and child advocates nurture and protect
those in their care.
We pray that our educators inspire children to develop childhood
memories and skills to lead others - making them good citizens, and as
Your children, that they project that image to future generations.
In thy name we pray!
Amen.

Good and Faithful Servants

Almighty God, heavenly father, we praise You and thank You for sending
us good and faithful servants.
It is right and just that we thank our educators for unselfishly dedicating their lives to
inspire and develop young minds. With special praise we ask for Your grace for teachers
working to show others the joy of giving to others by their chosen profession.
We pray to follow in their unmentioned and undesired fame as Rotarians dedicated to
serving others in our community and Your world.
We pray for Your guidance in all our projects that Rotarians be known as givers desiring
no credit for their work.
Amen.

Education Month

Let us pray,
Almighty God, as we enter the Rotary month dedicated to Education and literacy we
recall all in our past that have given us instruction in life.
That life that You have given us, oh Lord, compels Rotarians to do all we can to pass on to
generations following the knowledge so generously provided to us.
Current circumstances challenge our educators to a greater degree than the past. We pray
for their endurance and dedication to our students because it is all about them,
the student.
The love our educators give to those in their charge is evident in the success students
experience as they move on to new heights in leaning.
We pray that our community project and serve to inspire our teachers knowing that
Rotarians give as much support as is possible to provide.
In thy name we pray,
Amen.

Illumination

Let us pray,
We cast our worries before You o Lord with humility. We pray that You illuminate our
hearts and minds with the clarity only You can provide.
From Your Heavenly Sanctuary work in our lives, although we may be remote from each
other knowing that You are not remote from us.
Perhaps we have been lulled into a complacent place that threatens our worship of You.
Perhaps we have been distracted by things not essential to our faith in You.
Shower Rotarians with Your grace, sanctify us in the gifts You have given us.
As we Re-appraise our personal values and Renew our sense of purpose, may we
now long for closeness to You.
In thy name we pray,
Amen.

Equality

Let us Pray!
Almighty God, In Your eyes, all men (and women) are created equal. We are endowed by
You, our God, to promote the same kind of fairness to everyone.
Yes, we are provided by You with various abilities and talent to be used to support and
defend those less fortunate. Therefore, by combining our abilities,
It is right and just for Rotarians to accumulate knowledge of those oppressed and/or in
need and dispense our accumulated time, talent and treasure to help the welfare and
comfort for the greatest of those needs.
We pray for Your Holy Spirit to guide us to fulfill a complex mission with equality and
justice that we may satisfy Your will for us, and, to draw others to our mission.
In thy name we pray,
Amen.

Communication

Let us Pray!
Almighty God, we pray for those that struggle with the ability to communicate.
Rotarians are thankful for those that can inspire and generate enthusiasm among students
that wish to improve communication and language skills.
We ask that you inspire teachers to a calling to teach children, adults, the hearing, the
sight impaired and all that require individual and specialized attention.
As You motivate teachers and students to a better life, may they be thankful
enough to realize *Your* participation.
In Thy name we pray,
Amen

Vigilance

Let us pray,
Almighty God, As we recall that day almost 80 years ago that America was brutally
attacked without warning, our nation lost young people of principal and dedication.
By Your will, we pray now for vigilance against forces of evil and dedicate ourselves to
serving new generations as our means of strengthening our nation and community.
To those lost as they honored our country and us, they performed their Duty with a
courage born of the values You have given to all mankind. We pray, our God, to emulate
that courage and valor with our service.
Thru Rotary programs such as RLI, Youth Exchange,
S4TL, training and education, we pray for Your guidance as Rotarians salute those
lost by educating generations succeeding us.
In thy name we pray,
Amen.

Vocations

Let us Pray!

Almighty God, as we approach vocations and their value in our society,

we understand that vocations bear no partiality with You.

To discern what is valuable to the individual, we pray that You guide each person to

use the best of their talent with the desire for fulfillment in their vocation.

We pray that our vocational selection may be judged by You according to our works.

Amen.

4E. ENVIRONMENT

Environmental Balance

Almighty God!
As Rotarians we seek what is good, what is true and what is beautiful.
We reflect on the magnificent beauty in the world you have given us.
Rotarians pledge to protect and balance the beauty of Your Creation with the needs of
mankind and the depletion of resources which occurs for our progress.
You have given us Stewardship over our environment with the freedom to fruitfully
care for its majesty.
We pray for Your continued guidance to perform what is true and good in Your eyes.
In thy name we pray! Amen.

Core Value-Clean Water and Sanitation

Almighty God, we pray for continued Rotary success for clean water, sanitation, and
hygiene education as basic necessities for a healthy environment and a productive life.
We understand that when people have access to clean water and sanitation, waterborne
diseases decrease, children stay healthier and attend school more regularly, and mothers
can spend less time carrying water and more time helping their families.
We pray for Your inspiration and grace to help Rotarians mobilize resources, form
partnerships, and invest in infrastructure and training that yield long-term change
for clean water and sanitation.
In thy name we pray,
Amen.

Making a Difference

Let us Pray;
Almighty God, heavenly father, as we progress into the year of "Rotary Making a Difference" we pray for Your guidance.
We understand that one small effort by each one of us not only contributes, but that the whole is greater than the sum of its parts.
As we contribute our time, talent and treasure to the Rotary we love, pray that all who receive from us proceed to pass on what they have received.
May they be infused with the grace You have given Rotarians to achieve peace in the world.
Amen.

Community

Let us Pray,
Almighty God, we praise You and thank You for providing us with this wonderful world and beautiful community.
We pray for Your grace in protecting our citizens that they may be guided by our elected officials. Always knowing that You have provided us with life, liberty and the pursuit of happiness.

Our environment is a gift from You, and we pray for official guidance in the protection of what we have that inspires us to be part of this community.
In Thy name we pray,
Amen.

Living in Paradise

Let us Pray;
Almighty God, heavenly father, we appreciate living in this wonderful place, called paradise, that you have provided for us.
Instill in us the desire to preserve, protect and respect what we have as community.
You have given us the gift of a wonderful land to freely use as we please. As Rotarians, we can only give back to others for them to enjoy what we have.
With "Service above Self" we pray to be always mindful of You and what You desire for our fellow citizens.
In thy name we pray!
Amen.

4F. CHILD AND MATERNAL HEALTH

Children's Health

Let us Pray;
Almighty God, we thank You and pray to You for the health and safety of our children.
As Rotarians continue to give to causes to improve the lives of those generations
following, we ask for Your blessing on their efforts for self development. We also ask that
You continue to protect them in development of a health body, mind and spirit.
Rotarians continue to provide scholarships for their education. Rotarians seek to improve
children's health by eliminating disease and create good health habits. We turn to You to
instill in our children the spirit to develop Rotarian values and then pass on this Your will,
for all.
Our cause is Your cause. Give us the will to sacrifice what is necessary in the
development of future generations.
In thy name we pray,
Amen.

Children in Harm's Way

Let us Pray!
Almighty God, we pray for all children in harms way.
We ask Your intercession to rescue children that are at risk for survival
and are at the disposal of natural events.
For those that are actively involved in rescue efforts we pray that their
training and expertise may give them the motivation and dedication to
persevere and insure the safety of children.
As Rotarians, we pray that Your love envelop us to make sure that all
children can become good citizens and overcome conflict, disease, lack of
nutrition and poverty.
In Thy name we pray!
Amen.

Their Daily Bread

Let us pray;

Almighty God,

As Rotary promotes high-quality health care available to vulnerable mothers and
children, so they can live longer and grow stronger, we pray for Your grace.
In the name of the 5.9 million children under the age of five who die each year
because of malnutrition, inadequate health care, and poor sanitation — all of
which can be prevented, we pray that, at least locally, You empower those who
want to give them "their daily bread" with proper nutrition and health care.
As Rotarians, we recognize their heartfelt dedication and, in reflection of Your
will, we support their efforts.

In thy name we pray,

Amen.

4G. PEACE AND CONFLICT RESOLUTION

Designated Month

Let is Pray;

Almighty God, in this Rotary month dedicated to: "Peace and Conflict Resolution" we pray especially for peace in our families, our community, our nation and our world.

We hold great hope for the future of our great country and, in unison, we wish to join with others to promote Your principals in the joy of charity for all.

We pray that all here continue to put "service above self" and ask You to guide our efforts of enthusiasm for Rotary and our fellow citizens.

In Thy name we pray,

Amen.

Month of Rotary Focus

Let us Pray;

Almighty God,

as we conclude this month of Rotary's area of focus: Peace and Conflict Resolution.

We pray for your continued guidance as we demonstrate who we are.

We pledge to demonstrate Prudence and understanding of all points of view in discerning Your will.

As we Temper our response as an arbitrator or mediator we pledge to look deeper to harmonize with all.

Rotarians understand that justice is achieved in harmony with Your Will as we fortify a world with peace by our achievements in working for the greater good of all.

In thy name we pray,

Amen.

Leadership

Let us Pray; Almighty God.
We thank you for the opportunity of knowing You through Rotary.
As we climb the Rotary mountain to Peace and Conflict Resolution we ask for Your
support of those in Rotary who guide us, from our District and International leadership,
on this difficult trail.
The projects and help we give to others is in the same Spirit You give to us.
We accept every step of this journey as we are presented with new challenges, with the
Rotary spirit of a humble soul and a tender heart.
In Thy name we pray.
Amen

Making a Difference

Let us Pray;
Almighty God, heavenly father, as we progress into the year of "Rotary
Making a Difference" we pray for Your guidance.
We understand that one small effort by each one of us not only
contributes, but that the whole is greater than the sum of its parts.
As we contribute our time, talent and treasure to the Rotary we love, pray
that all who receive from us proceed to pass on what they have received.
May they be infused with the grace You have given Rotarians to achieve
peace in the world.
Amen.

Senseless Acts of Violence

Let us Pray;

Almighty God. As Rotarians we pursue "Peace and Conflict Resolution" and
find it hard to justify senseless acts of violence by others.
Rotarians can hope that by making lives better throughout the world, we are
doing Your work and that peace will be achieved.
We pray for the souls of victims of violence - that they be with You.
We pray for the fortitude You provide us, and that Your justice will prevail.
Amen.

Population Displacement

Let us Pray!

Almighty God, As conflict and violence displace millions of people each year, we pray to
You for their safety and care.
We pray because half of those killed in conflict are children, and 90 percent are civilians.
As Rotarians, we cannot accept conflict as a way of life.
We pray to continue our Rotary projects to provide training that fosters understanding
and provides others with the skills to resolve conflicts.
Through our service projects, peace fellowships, and scholarships, we ask for Your
council as our members take action to address the underlying causes of conflict, including
poverty, inequality, ethnic tension, lack of access to education, and unequal
distribution of resources.
In thy name we pray,
Amen.

Persecution

Let us Pray;
Almighty God, we deeply pray for those who suffer because of the faith they have in You.
We pray that their persecution at the hands of others will not become a sacrifice.
As Rotarians, we can only continue our charity and love for those oppressed around the
world and give of ourselves for their health and comfort.
Please give us the strength to overlook the injustice perpetrated by oppressors and
proceed to reconcile, through charity, the dangers to world peace.
Amen.

Life in Harms Way

Let us pray,
Almighty God,
We, Your people, are engulfed in great tragedy and trial.
There are those far away that are looking for hope of survival as we lay secure
in relative safety.
Our collective prayer is for their welfare and safety.
We know not life in harm's way.
We do not live in
the privation, desolation and lack of security they experience.
Evil and oppression surround them directly at every moment without regard
for human life. They feel only the weight of subjugation and eventual death.
We ask that You, our God, purge the fear, anxiety, frustration and sense of
abandonment they now experience.
We pray especially for the women and all children in harms way.
We ask Your intercession to rescue those that are at risk for survival and are at
the disposal of these unnatural events.
For those that are actively involved in rescue efforts we pray that their training
and expertise may give them the will, motivation and dedication to persevere
and insure safety and a life that You promise.
As You have done so often, we pray You convert evil and oppression without
their sacrifice.
As Rotarians, may we envelope Your ideals in prayer that the prayer for peace
may envelope all.
In Thy name we pray!
Amen.

Quest for Peace

Let us Pray;

Almighty God, as Rotarians we ask for your guidance in our quest for peace:
Peace in our homes, community, nation and in the world.
Peace for those in need that they may have enough food, clothing and shelter.
Peace through knowing that our health and the health of others is secure.
And, peace in knowing that you are there to protect all from harm.

Amen.

Not to Condemn

Let us Pray!

Almighty God, bless us with the resolve to resist the temptation to
condemn those that would persecute and subjugate others.
We pray that freedom of conscience prevails throughout the world as it
does in areas of a Rotary presence.
Lord, we pray for the discipline and dedication to persevere in the Rotary
Area of Focus of: Peace and Conflict Resolution.
For those displaced, and because all are created in Your image, we pray for
their family unity and their safety and that they may enjoy the joyful
harmony of Your grace as they seek a better life.

Amen.

Political Considerations

Let us Pray;

Almighty God, one of Rotary's principal goals is Peace and Conflict Resolution.
We pray for your guidance that we may, perhaps, over-ride political considerations as
we generate goodwill in our community and in our International
relations.
Consider our International Project in helping us to establish that goodwill with our
partner's and their
Rotary Club.
Be with us throughout, that we may all project our heartfelt nature in this, Your
Rotary world.
Amen.

Dissimilar Views

Let us Pray;

Almighty God; In our time, we have been blessed by You with those who
give us lasting inspiration to achieve peace and to resolve conflicts.
Many find difficulty when confronted with dissimilar views and
impatiently react, escalating the conflict.
We pray for Your consolation and guidance as we practice patience with
others. We understand that prudence and faith in You will enable a
temperate response to anger and that true justice may be served.
In thy name we pray.
Amen.

Faith

Let us Pray;
Almighty God, we deeply pray for those who suffer because of the faith they
have in You. We pray that their persecution at the hands of others will not
become a sacrifice.
As Rotarians, we can only continue our charity and love for those oppressed
around the world and give of ourselves for their health and comfort.
Please give us the strength to overlook the injustice perpetrated by oppressors
and proceed to reconcile, through charity, the dangers to world peace.
Amen.

Service Above Self

Let is Pray;
Almighty God, at this time of year we pray especially for the core Rotary effort of peace
and the resolution of conflicts throughout the world.
We hold great hope for the future of our great country and, in unison, we wish to join
with others to promote Your principals in the joy of charity for all.
We pray that all here continue to put "service above self" and guide our efforts with
enthusiasm for Rotary and our fellow citizens throughout the world.
Amen.

The Least of These

Let us Pray!

Almighty God, heavenly father. We pray for the peace and security of "The least of these our brethren"!

From our perch of relative safety, we reflect on those who may be persecuted and who are living in fear for themselves, and the ones they love and are responsible for.

We pray that You may comfort and give them hope. That they see clearly that there are many outside of their own view that are praying with them for our redemption in this world and elevation to Your heavenly kingdom.

We pray that Rotary may be the vehicle of truth and compassion for their peace.

Amen.

Unity

Let us Pray;

Almighty God; "Source of all goodness", we look to You for inspiration to challenge persecution and exploitation of our brothers and sisters.

Conform us to Your will for all that You may want for a world in peace.

Give us the strength, through our service, to transform division to unity and differences of opinion to Your will.

In thy name we pray.

Amen.

Unity

Let us Pray!
As we join together as fellow Rotarians we praise You for the unity You have given us.
The unity of clubs and districts give us the strength to endure the small hardships *we* have
in order to help the greater hardships of others.
In this Rotary month of recognizing "Peace and Conflict Resolution" **all** Rotarians
understand that "Peace thru Service" can only be achieved with *Your* guidance and grace.
We pray for the fortitude to persevere in our service to achieve peace in our homes, our
community and our world.
In **Thy** name we pray,
Amen.

Health and Water

Let Us Pray!
Almighty God, as we work for Rotary's goal of Peace and Conflict Resolution, we pray not
to lose sight of those components under the control You have given us.
We pray that our educational programs be always in your sight that by Your reason we
may influence those in our care and guidance to be good citizens of our community, their
country and Your world.
By Rotary Health and Water programs we pray that successes are fruitful in removing
nation and personal barriers in the underdeveloped world for the greater security of all.
In Thy name we pray!
Amen.

Holy Week

Let us Pray!
Almighty God, we thank You for the many gifts you have given us this year.
The greatest gift we can receive is the hope You give us for a peaceful world. A
world here on earth that is equal to our ultimate gift of heaven.
As we attend our Rotarian duties in the coming year, we pray for Your
guidance to ensure cooperation with others because there needs are not
always our needs.
We pray that the best of our mutual efforts be found by working together.
Amen!

Home and Community

Let us Pray;
Almighty God, as Rotarians we ask for your guidance in our quest for peace:
Peace in our homes, community, nation and in the world.
Peace for those in need that they may have enough food, clothing and shelter.
Peace through knowing that our health and the health of others is secure.
And, peace in knowing that you are there to protect all from harm.
Amen.

Pastoral Virtues

As we conclude this month of Rotary's area of focus: Peace and Conflict Resolution.
We pray for your continued guidance as we demonstrate who we are.
We pledge to demonstrate Prudence and understanding of all points of view in
discerning Your will.
As we Temper our response as an arbitrator or mediator we pledge to look deeper to
harmonize with all.
Rotarians understand that justice is achieved in harmony with Your Will as we fortify
a world with peace by our achievements in working for the greater good of all.
In thy name we pray,
Amen.

Peace Through Service

Let us Pray!
As we join together as fellow Rotarians we praise You for the unity You
have given us.
The unity of clubs and districts give us the strength to endure the small
hardships *we* have in order to help the greater hardships of others.
In this Rotary month of recognizing "Peace and Conflict Resolution" **all**
Rotarians understand that "Peace thru Service" can only be achieved with
Your guidance and grace.
We pray for the fortitude to persevere in our service to achieve peace in
our homes, our community and our world.
In **Thy** name we pray,
Amen.

Peace thru Service

Let us Pray!
Almighty God, As conflict and violence displace millions of people each year,
we pray to You for their safety and care.
We pray because half of those killed in conflict are children, and 90 percent
are civilians. As Rotarians, we cannot accept conflict as a way of life.
We pray to continue our Rotary projects to provide training that fosters
understanding and provides others with the skills to resolve conflicts.
Through our service projects, peace fellowships, and scholarships, we ask for
Your council as our members take action to address the underlying causes of
conflict, including poverty, inequality, ethnic tension, lack of access to
education, and unequal distribution of resources.
In thy name we pray,
Amen.

Challenge

Let us Pray;
Almighty God; "Source of all goodness", we look to You for inspiration to
challenge persecution and exploitation of our brothers and sisters.
Conform us to Your will for all that You may want for a world in peace.
Give us the strength, through our service, to transform division to unity
and differences of opinion to Your will.
In thy name we pray.
Amen.

Resolve

Let us Pray!
Almighty God, bless us with the resolve to resist those that would persecute and subjugate others.
We pray that freedom of conscience prevails throughout the world as it does in areas of a Rotary presence, and in those areawhere Rotary does not exist, we pray that governments may look upon Rotary as a blessing for their people.
Lord, we pray for the discipline and dedication to persevere in the Rotary Area of Focus of: Peace and Conflict Resolution.
For those displaced, and because all are created in Your image, we pray for their family unity and their safety and that they may enjoy the joyful harmony of Your grace as they seek a better life.
Amen.

Peace on Earth Goodwill Toward Men

Let us pray:
Almighty God, heavenly father
We reflect on the birth of a child in this season of hope, and pray for "peace on earth goodwill to men".
As Rotarians, we follow the Rotary action plan for peace on earth. We pray to you for guidance that we may follow this plan for our service to those less fortunate.
Almighty God, you have empowered us with intelligence and the will to achieve Your goals. As we embrace this Rotary area of focus and tradition, we pray for success in achieving the Peace and Conflict Resolution promised to us by You in sacred scripture.
Guide us to reach out to others, to take action, to become involved in meaningful plans to improve the lives of others.
We pray for the peace of this season to overwhelm us that we may positively influence others to work with us and bring "peace on earth" to all mankind.
In thy name we pray,
Amen.

Give Unto Others

Let us pray,

Almighty God,

Rotarians pledge to acknowledge and question in our daily life: Is it "Fair to all Concerned"?

Our efforts are such as to render superficial those differences that may divide us.

You, our God, have taught us to "give unto others". We do not dwell on or wonder what others are made of. We only need to know what are their needs.

Rotarians accept our common challenges and take refuge in the good that comes to others from our efforts.

As we go thru our daily life we pledge not to define or delineate our differences, but rather work towards common goals and "Peace Thru Service".

Inspire in us the confidence to celebrate our diversity and inclusion.

In thy name we pray,

Amen.

Veterans

Let us Pray!

Almighty God, this nation thrives because of the service of our Armed Forces Veterans.

Their sacrifices have protected our freedoms, our families and our America.

We pray that this nation continue to respect and support what veterans have won in battle against continued evolving evil.

We pray You heal those that suffer from their sacrifice.

We ask that You comfort those left behind while they defend us.

For the families of those lost, may they know, that Rotarians support and love them as they grieve their loss.

As Rotarians pursue Peace and Conflict Resolution,

we pray for the time of judgement when: "One nation shall not raise the sword against another, nor shall they train for war again".

In thy name we pray,

Amen.

Erasing Fear

Let us Pray!

Almighty God,

We pray to you to erase the fear and tension between people.

As Rotarians we are called to reflect Your infinite compassion for us and evangelize the Rotary Principal of "Peace thru Service".

As we Work to Resolve Conflict between all people, we pray to You, with sincerity of mind and purpose, for the ability to reason for ourselves and, with others, to change the hearts of those troubled souls that deny the Right to Life and Freedom.

For compassion for those oppressed and the need for order, as You have ordered the universe, we pray You give us a spirit of confidence to overcome our differences with goals and purpose for all to work to achieve life, liberty and happiness. Knowing that true peace and happiness come from serving others for You.

In thy name we pray,

Amen.

Holy Season

Let us pray!

We ask You to continue to pour Your grace on Rotarians as we proceed in our programs promoting world peace.

During this Holy Season we pray that all may see the value of others.

Especially their adversaries.

The standards You have set for Your people are high considering our human frailty.

As we place You above all others, we ask that all may be joined together in Your name as the spirit of this season comes into our hearts.

Amen.

Conflict Resolution

Let us Pray!
Almighty God, we praise you and thank you for providing Rotary with giving Rotarians and those who look to you for counsel as our leaders.
Where there is hunger and poverty there are Rotarians.
Where there is weather disasters there are Rotarians.
Where education is needed there are Rotarians.
Where health problems exist Rotarians volunteer.
Conflict resolution causes Rotarians to volunteer because we believe in "Peace thru Service".

We continue to pray for Your guidance to our leadership that all may enjoy the love You inspire.
Amen

Good Over Evil

Let us pray.
Almighty God, we pray for all who give to make this a better world. Evil cannot prevail from the weight of all who do good.
"A greater love hath no man than to lay down his life for a friend."
We cannot do it all and need partners. It is up to everyone to project the ideals of Rotary to balance the acts of those with the evil that we see and we must recruit others to those ideals.
We pray that our love of You, our God, as it is ever present in Your Spirit within us, can and must overwhelm those that seek to oppress others.
As Rotary works on the outskirts of evil events, we pray our efforts go deeper to those we serve and pray that society everywhere may be transformed to a just and peaceful world.
Amen.

4H. DISASTER RESPONSE

Calamities

Let us pray!
Almighty God, heavenly father we are extremely thankful for the grace
You have bestowed on us. We are thankful that the extreme destruction of
our precious island did not occur.
We are thankful for the inspiration and dedication of those who respond
with necessary services.
As we adjust to the calamities our community has experienced, we pray
for Your continued grace as we recover.
We pray to remember those less fortunate to bring their lives back to
normal. The struggle they pursue is perhaps more severe than our own.
We pray that the giving nature of Rotarians in our community remain an
inspiration to all.
In thy name we pray!
Amen.

In Response to Covid-19

Almighty God, our hope is in you.
We take to heart your abundant grace and invocation to
"Be not afraid". In our time of crisis, in this period of our isolation from one
another, we pray to continue our Rotary mission of improving health and
disease prevention in a troubled world.
We pray for those in need of the hope that You provide. Take those who
succumb to disease into Your heavenly home.
May those that become infected be imbued with the hope and optimism that
faith in You provide for their healing.
For caregivers, who selflessly put themselves in harms way, we pray that You
help them maintain their sense of mission with dedication and enthusiasm
because they have the ability to inspire all.
As we take measures to meet our mission, we pray to use collective Rotary
minds and intellect to find ways to communicate mission as a great challenge.
In this time of crisis we pray for the enthusiasm to stick to our cause.
As your humble servants, we understand that communication through our
prayer to You is the greatest communication.
In thy name we pray,
Amen.

Hero's Song

Let us pray;
Songs are sung of hero's past, of those distinguished in battle, or elevated to great position.
But what of the great mass of mankind who, by God's grace, performed with valor, honor and without the glory of worldly recognition.
Those that did what had to be done in their time and in a way that gives glory to God: unselfish and tempered by their time. Those unsung.
They live today, in a different way, a different place, as warriors in public service and are spontaneous in doing right in a time of crisis.
They have learned to do right sometimes by how they were brought up and then through training. They live among us.
Respect and honor. Unselfish. Hero's are not to be worshiped, they do not care to be worshiped. If ego exists in the hero, question whether they are hero's?
Duty, honor, country, community.
The live where dedication to duty is distinctive and valor is common.
Where their working realm is a zone apart, not to be pierced by outside thought.
The hero mocks the self proclaimed by his humility, his simple act of not reacting in his own self interest. He does not proclaim he is the greatest, the best. Those that are self adorned.
His cause is not himself.
The hero does and walks away. He hides in the comfort of duty performed.
In thy name we pray,
Amen.

Memorium

Let us Pray;
Almighty God, we praise you and thank you for your everlasting care.
Thy will be done.
As a nation in mourning, we are coming to terms with horrific tragedy close to us and pray to understand.
As You, our God, knows the plan You have established, we pray to believe and understand that whatever occurs in our world on Earth has a glorious future for those who believe in You.
We pray for the souls who perish through evil. May you take them into your heavenly kingdom.
We pray for consolation in the hearts of those who are closest to those perished with reconciliation and recognition of You in Your infinite wisdom.
Theirs is a living legacy for which we will always thank You: for their service and inspiration.
Amen.

Let us Pray;

Almighty God, we praise you and thank you for your everlasting care.

Thy will be done.

As a nation in mourning, we are coming to terms with horrific tragedy in the midwest and pray to understand.

As You, our God, knows the plan You have established, we pray to believe and understand that whatever occurs in our world on Earth has a glorious future for those who believe in You.

We pray for the souls who perish through these sudden events. May you take them into your heavenly kingdom.

We pray for consolation in the hearts of those who are closest to those perished with reconciliation and recognition of You in Your infinite wisdom.

We pray for those who serve to re-establish the living conditions of communities tragically degraded and lost. As Rotarians assist in these efforts we ask for Your grace.

Theirs is a living legacy for which we will always thank You: for their service and inspiration.

Amen.

Consolation

Let us Pray;

Almighty God, heavenly father, we praise You and thank You for sending us good and faithful servants.

As we celebrate today those you have taken into Your heavenly home, we pray to remember their deeds and accomplishments in their acts of Sainthood.

We pray to follow in their unmentioned and undesired fame as Rotarians dedicated to serving others in our community and Your world.

We pray for Your guidance in all our projects that Rotarians be known as givers desiring no credit for their work.

Amen.

Legacy

Let is Pray;
Almighty God, heavenly father, we pray for the care of those who have
preceded us in life.
As we remember their example and contributions
to our society we pray that You protect and prolong their life, with quality, as
they proceed to You in their heavenly home.
For those that dedicate themselves to the care of those passing through life, we
pray for their continued passion in passing on Your empathy and love.
Amen.

Losing a Brother

Let us Pray!
We are in awe of the gifts You have given us.
When we lose a brother, we reflect and thank those that have dedicated their lives and
have continued to serve You, our community and ourselves by selflessly participating in
building our community from the beginning to the greatness that it has become.
In the process of creation, we take You as our guide. In the small ways we, in our
humanity, participate in creativity we thank and honor those, by Your grace, that have
used their creative ability to think of others before themselves and give us the unique
pride and comfort of our community.
In thy name we pray,
Amen.

Decline

Let us Pray!
Almighty God and father of all, as Rotarians we continue to
experience the decline of our loved ones.
We do pray for their recovery and realize their slow departure
from us and their welcome by You.
We pray for those that see to their welfare and show with loving
care respect as they share in their memories together.
As a family of Rotarians, we pray to share with the caregivers
among us their loving experience.
In Thy name we pray,
Amen.

911 Memorial

Let us pray,
Almighty God, As we approach yet another anniversary of tragedy and
evil perpetrated against others in humanity we remember all those lost
and pray they are now in Your care.
For those we knew who perished on 9/11/2001, let us now recall their
names and their families:

I remember: _____

Anyone else? _____

For all those lost and those left to grieve we pray for Your consolation in
helping them heal.
We praise You, Almighty God, for those that sacrificed and who gave of
themselves to prove the heroism and goodwill in helping heal the great
wound created.
Rotarians pray for Peace and Resolution of Conflicts. Please protect us, O
God, from all those who wish to inflict harm on others. May Rotarians
become the engine of a world at peace.
In thy name we pray,
Amen.

911 Memorial

Let us pray,
Almighty God, It is appropriate today that Rotarians dwell on the tragic lose of our youth with a brutal attack on our country and how we can honor their memory. With their exuberant youth they chose to serve - as Rotarians choose to serve.
By Your will, we pray now for vigilance against forces of evil and dedicate ourselves to serving new generations as **our** means of strengthening our nation and community. To those lost as they honored our country and us, they performed their Duty with a courage born of the values You have given to all mankind. We pray, our God, with our hope in You, to emulate that courage and valor with **our** service to perpetuate their memory.
Thru Rotary programs such as Interact, Rotaract, Youth Exchange, S4TL, training and education, we pray for Your guidance as Rotarians salute those lost by educating generations succeeding us.
In thy name we pray,
Amen.

Empathy for Others

Let us pray!
As we make our way through this life we sometimes need to be awakened from our own problems to finally realize that we long to see your face and are not alone.
As we are accustomed to our comfortable life in paradise, there are others, Rotarians work to reach, that require assistance for the very basics in life.
As we practice to understand their plight we ask for Your guidance and grace to truly understand their needs.
We pray that Rotarians work in harmony that we may assist those in need.
In thy name we pray!
Amen

Personal Tragedy

Let us Pray!
We all feel the pain of tragedy to our fellow man and often wonder
why bad things happen to good people.
As Rotarians we see many tragedies and conflicts in Your world that we can only offer our
small part in making life easier and worthwhile for those in need.
There is no satisfaction in tragedy and we pray that there be some consolation for the
victims and their loved ones in knowing that others are thinking and
praying for their healing.
Bad things happen and we recognize that You, our God, is with us in promoting the good
and beauty by unifying us in the knowledge of Your loving kindness to all.
In thy name we pray,
Amen.

Nation in Mourning

Let us Pray!
Almighty God, we praise you and thank you for your everlasting care. Thy
will be done.
As a nation in mourning, we are coming to terms with horrific tragedy
close to us and pray to understand.
As You, our God, knows the plan You have established, we pray to believe
and understand that whatever occurs in our world on Earth has a glorious
future for those who believe in You.
We pray for the souls who perish through evil. May you take them into
your heavenly kingdom.
We pray for consolation in the hearts of those who are closest to those
perished with reconciliation and recognition of You in Your infinite
wisdom. Amen.

Natural Disaster

Let us pray!
Almighty God, heavenly father we are extremely thankful for the grace
You have bestowed on us. We are thankful that the extreme destruction of
our precious island did not occur.
We are thankful for the inspiration and dedication of those who respond
with necessary services.
As we adjust to the calamities our community has experienced, we pray
for Your continued grace as we recover.
We pray to remember those less fortunate to bring their lives back to
normal. The struggle they pursue is perhaps more severe than our own.
We pray that the giving nature of Rotarians in our community remain an
inspiration to all.
In thy name we pray!
Amen.

Anniversary Day (District Meeting 5/13/18)

Let us pray!
This is a day we remember as a horror for the loss of so many worthy souls
innocently taken from us.
In their innocence, however, their sacrifice has given us unity in Your
name. The determination shown in the recovery from the evil is worthy of
all that You have given us as a people and reinforces the Rotary principal
of: Service Above Self".
We pray that as we remember the events of that day and the loss of our
friends, we may continue to perform as Rotarians in unity with all that
suffered loss on that day.
In thy name we pray!
Amen.

Personal

Let us Pray!
We all feel the pain of tragedy to our fellow man and often wonder why
bad things happen to good people.
As Rotarians we see many tragedies and conflicts in Your world that we
can only offer our small part in making life easier and worthwhile for
those in need.
There is no satisfaction in tragedy and we pray that there be some
consolation for the victims and their loved ones in knowing that others are
thinking and praying for their healing.
Bad things happen and we recognize that You, our God, is with us in
promoting the good and beauty by unifying us in the knowledge of Your
loving kindness to all.
In thy name we pray,
Amen.

5. ASSEMBLY

Grain of Sand

Let us pray,
Almighty God:
Help us to overcome the feeling that we are only one grain of sand in
a great world of needs.
Yes, we are but one grain of Rotary sand in a global network of 1.2 million neighbors,
friends, leaders, and problem-solvers who see a world where people unite and take
action to create lasting change – across the globe.
We ask You to continue to inspire Rotarians to use imagination and vision to dedicate
the variety of talents You have given us to form a beachhead against the wave of
intolerance and apathy towards our fellow citizens of the world.
As waves follow waves coming to a beach, we pray for a new great wave of goodness,
and new Rotary sand, by the building of so many missions designed to improve the
lives of those less fortunate, that we overwhelm the world in order
that evil must decline.
May each grain of sand new and old, follow Your word in a spirit of humility and
perseverance born of Your love for us.
In thy name we pray,
Amen.

Club (District)

DISTRICT ASSEMBLY - APRIL 25, 2020

Let us pray;
Almighty God, You are our refuge. You are our strength!
By Your grace, we are thankful for Your giving mankind the intelligence and will to develop
systems to assemble without personal contact - which we dearly miss.
By our Covenant with You, our God, You have given us the mission that we will be your
people with instruction to serve the "least of these our brethren".
We, as Rotarians, act with solidarity, and, with this strength, You give us greater
power to serve others.
As with the great Rotary effort to eradicate Polio, we accept the current crisis as only a
deviation from that mission and accept the additional calling.
Our Rotarian prayer is that, with this current crisis, Your Suffering Servants are inspired to
holiness in Your kingdom here on Earth as we hope to enter Your kingdom in Heaven.
The Polio **Plus** rallying cry is our call to action and a way for Rotarians to serve You better
and more completely.
Guide us with Your grace.
In Thy name we pray,
Amen.

Good Council

Let us pray;
Dear Lord, as we gather in assembly, we pray to You to instill in us the
best of intentions in fulfilling Rotary ideals.
We have no problem in remembering the: "Four Way Test" or "Service
Above Self" when we are assembled here.
As You are aware, it sometimes becomes difficult to remember those
messages in our daily activities.
We pray that You be with us perpetually, as counsel, as we go thru
everyday life because Your principals are Rotary principals.
Amen.

New Life

Let Us Pray!
Almighty God, we are joined here together in Your name to transfer our clubs leadership.
We pray for the continuity of the past with the core values You have given us.
As You have provided the seed of new life from the present we see that even in the death
of life, new spirit, new life develops.
The establishment of our Rotary club as among the vast amalgam of a worldwide
congregation of members serving mankind, provides the energy and way for us to thrive.
Where others see problems, Rotarians see opportunity to serve others,
Where others see obstacles, Rotarians are energized by humanities needs for faith,
hope and charity.
As the previous administrations of our club provide the seed of new life in Rotary, we
pray that our club may flourish in the same joy You have provided for us from the past.
We thank You, Almighty God, for continuity and the continuation of Rotary tradition,
realizing that "Service Above Self" is serving You.
Amen.

Change of Leadership

Let us pray!
As we celebrate our nations independence we recall that we are
"One Nation Under God".
We recall all of the benefits You have given us as we are able to pursue life,
liberty and happiness.
We pray our Representative Republic always remembers why freedom
is so important.
As Rotarians, we have the freedom to choose those we wish to help and pray Your
grace permits us to choose wisely.
As the "torch is passed" and our new Board takes effect, we pray that Rotary
generosity continues this year in its dedication to our areas of focus: to build
international relationships, improve lives, and create a better world to support our
peace efforts and end polio forever.
We pray for Your guidance as Rotarians project these American values for others.
In Thy name we pray!
Amen.

Club (District) Assembly

From Sunrise Rotary meeting of 4/13/21 and District Conference of 4/17/21

Let us pray, Almighty God:
You have taught us that: "a house divided against itself cannot stand".
As we see in our time an effort for the division of societal components, we understand
that we cannot seek peace if we make war with each other. We pray You give us the
strength to avoid anything that brings discord.
Bind us closely, as Paul Harris and his associates designed Rotary. May we remain
instruments of Unity in a world torn by differences.
May our Unity of body, mind and spirit, of one heart and soul,
remain with ourselves, our club and Rotary with an attitude born of charity.
We seek to be better as we imitate Your love for us, even if we see no response. By Your
grace, the great Rotary tree of hope, united in charity, with our faith in You our good
God, we pray to enjoy good health of spirit.
With patience and forbearance for others and an understanding of their needs, we pray to
overcome all barriers and differences whether they be: social, economic, racial or cultural.
Charity, like music for the soul, unites us.
In thy name we pray.
Amen.

Club Goals

Let us Pray!

Almighty God, we humbly pray for Your guidance in the coming new year.
We realize that this club has been very aggressive in pursuit of goals that challenge us every day.

We pray that our goals are just and pleasing in Your eyes that they may ultimately bring peace and comfort to those receiving aid.

Please help us to retain the joy and discipline necessary to reach our club's and Rotary goals and to serve others.

Amen

6. COMMUNITY

Relationships

Let us Pray!
Oh Lord, we praise you and thank you for giving us the relationships we have
through Rotary.
We know that we can only do so much for others by ourselves.
We understand that by combining our Rotary relationships here on Marco Island,
that we can provide much more for those in need.
With our District and International relationships we can greatly increase our
efforts for a world in great need.
We thank You for the blessing of the sum of our efforts in defining common goals
and reaching out to others.
We pray that with Your help, our combined relationships can impact: elimination
of disease, provide clean water and nutrition, promote education and advance the
nobility of Your people.
Amen

Caring Community

Let us Pray;
Almighty God, heavenly father, we thank you for our caring community.
When we visit a merchant, our sense of agreement, cooperation and
willingness to work with us is far beyond what we may have experienced
wherever our residence was before.
When we ask for their cooperation in our programs and efforts may we
continue to sense a connection and an enthusiasm to help.
Our humility on acceptance brings us together as one and we thank You
for this community unity.
As your Holy Spirit prevails among us in our Rotary efforts, we pray for
humility in acceptance and may we always be reminded that our values
and Yours are one.
Amen.

Living in Paradise

Let us Pray;
Almighty God, heavenly father, we appreciate living in this wonderful
place, called paradise, that you have provided for us.
Instill in us the desire to preserve, protect and respect what we have as
community with Rotary unity and due fellowship.
You have given us the gift of a wonderful land to freely use as we please.
As Rotarians, we can only give back to others as You have guided us, for
them to enjoy what we have.
With "Service above Self" we pray to be always mindful of You and what
You desire for our fellow citizens.
In thy name we pray!
Amen.

Calamities

Let us pray!
Almighty God, heavenly father we are extremely thankful for the grace
You have bestowed on us. We are thankful that the extreme destruction of
our precious island did not occur.
We are thankful for the inspiration and dedication of those who respond
with necessary services.
As we adjust to the calamities our community has experienced, we pray
for Your continued grace as we recover.
We pray to remember those less fortunate to bring their lives back to
normal. The struggle they pursue is perhaps more severe than our own.
We pray that the giving nature of Rotarians in our community remain an
inspiration to all.
In thy name we pray!
Amen.

Those Less Fortunate

Let us Pray!
May we never forget Your goodness in helping us to provide for our families.
As we face our daily trials in this sweet land of liberty let us recall, each day, the
overwhelming trials of other families in a world that does not have liberty or, the ability to
grow in the same kind of peace and prosperity we enjoy.
Since Rotary gives us the ability to help those less fortunate, may we project the values
You have given us as Americans, with the same joy we have in our own families.
In Your name we pray!
Amen.

Elected Officials

Let us Pray,
Almighty God, we praise You and thank You for providing us with this
wonderful world and beautiful community.
We pray for Your grace in protecting our citizens that they may be guided
by our elected officials. Always knowing that You have provided us with
life, liberty and the pursuit of happiness.
Our environment is a gift from You, and we pray for official guidance in
the protection of what we have that inspires us to be part of this
community.
In Thy name we pray,
Amen.

7. DISASTER RESPONSE

Calamities

Let us pray!
Almighty God, heavenly father we are extremely thankful for the grace
You have bestowed on us. We are thankful that the extreme destruction of
our precious island did not occur.
We are thankful for the inspiration and dedication of those who respond
with necessary services.
As we adjust to the calamities our community has experienced, we pray
for Your continued grace as we recover.
We pray to remember those less fortunate to bring their lives back to
normal. The struggle they pursue is perhaps more severe than our own.
We pray that the giving nature of Rotarians in our community remain an
inspiration to all.
In thy name we pray!
Amen.

In Response to Covid-19

Almighty God, our hope is in you.
We take to heart your abundant grace and invocation to
"Be not afraid". In our time of crisis, in this period of our isolation from one
another, we pray to continue our Rotary mission of improving health and disease
prevention in a troubled world.
We pray for those in need of the hope that You provide. Take those who succumb
to disease into Your heavenly home.
May those that become infected be imbued with the hope and optimism that faith
in You provide for their healing.
For caregivers, who selflessly put themselves in harms way, we pray that You help
them maintain their sense of mission with dedication and enthusiasm because
they have the ability to inspire all.
As we take measures to meet our mission, we pray to use collective Rotary minds
and intellect to find ways to communicate mission as a great challenge. In this
time of crisis we pray for the enthusiasm to stick to our cause.
As your humble servants, we understand that communication through our prayer
to You is the greatest communication.
In thy name we pray,
Amen.

8. ENVIRONVMENT

Stewardship

Let us pray;
Almighty God!
As Rotarians we seek what is good, what is true and what is beautiful.
We reflect on the magnificent beauty in the world you have given us.
Rotarians pledge to protect and balance the beauty of Your Creation with the needs of mankind and the depletion of resources which occurs for our progress.
You have given us Stewardship over our environment with the freedom to fruitfully care for its majesty.
We pray for Your continued guidance to perform what is true and good in Your eyes.
In thy name we pray!
Amen.

Child Care

Let us Pray,
Almighty God,
We pray that caregivers, teachers and child advocates nurture and protect those in their care.

We pray that our educators inspire children to develop childhood memories and skills to lead others - making them good citizens, and as Your children, that they project that image to future generations.
In thy name we pray!
Amen.

Teachers

Let us Pray;
Almighty God, heavenly father, we praise You and thank You for sending us good and faithful servants.
It is right and just that we thank our educators for unselfishly dedicating their lives to inspire and develope young minds. With special praise we ask for Your grace for teachers working to show others the joy of giving to others by their chosen profession.
We pray to follow in their unmentioned and undesired fame as Rotarians dedicated to serving others in our community and Your world.
We pray for Your guidance in all our projects that Rotarians be known as givers desiring no credit for their work.
Amen.

9. EQUALITY

In Perpetuity

Let Us Pray!
Almighty God, we are forever grateful for the infusion of Your and
American principles of Liberty, Justice and the industry to pass on to all
the world these ideals through Rotary.
We thank You for providing us with the ability to work, with Your Grace,
and give others incentive by helping them to improve their lives.
The infection of Your principals provide American Rotarians with
necessary pride to perpetuate giving to others and dedicate each Club to
make this a better world by our service.
Amen.

Love

Let Us Pray!
Almighty God, we are endowed by You with the qualities of faith, hope and love.
As we pursue our love for You, Rotarians naturally evolve into pursuing love for
our fellow man and charity for others.
Rotarians see, as You referred to them as: "the least of these our brethren", as a
quest for equality for them in their way of life. As they may seem to be of less
economic stature, Rotarians ask for Your guidance to raise all to a status that gives
them hope by faith in You.
We pray that our every effort to improve quality of life throughout the world, and
especially in our community, be blessed by our God that we may have the energy
and will to understand their needs and work to improve their quality of life.
In thy name we pray,
Amen.

Moral Progress

Let us Pray!
Our Lord and Our God,
We understand that if we are to morally progress in our culture, we can only accomplish this with the guidance and grace You give us.
To compromise and interject our own objectives only dilute Your efforts, and we Your people, cannot fully accomplish what the Rotary world is capable of.
We understand that the world of giving back to others is what please You.
Rotarians are dedicated this effort.
In thy name we pray,
Amen.

Developing Facilities

Almighty God,
We pray for the necessary empathy for the millions of people worldwide in misery, pain, and poverty with resultant disease.
As Rotarians we all need to mobilize our concern for those afflicted with disease.
Give us the strength and fortitude to educate and participate, in each our small way, to lead in the development of clinics, facilities and personnel in underserved communities struggling with outbreaks.
We pray for Your guidance in turning Rotary empathy into meaningful mobilization.
In Thy name we pray,
Amen.

In Response to Covid-19

Almighty God, our hope is in you.
We take to heart your abundant grace and invocation to
"Be not afraid". In our time of crisis, in this period of our isolation from one
another, we pray to continue our Rotary mission of improving health and
disease prevention in a troubled world.
We pray for those in need of the hope that You provide. Take those who
succumb to disease into Your heavenly home.
May those that become infected be imbued with the hope and optimism that
faith in You provide for their healing.
For caregivers, who selflessly put themselves in harms way, we pray that You
help them maintain their sense of mission with dedication and enthusiasm
because they have the ability to inspire all.
As we take measures to meet our mission, we pray to use collective Rotary
minds and intellect to find ways to communicate mission as a great challenge.
In this time of crisis we pray for the enthusiasm to stick to our cause.
As your humble servants, we understand that communication through our
prayer to You is the greatest communication.
In thy name we pray,
Amen.

Fortitude

Let us Pray;
If not for You, Almighty God, mankind could not have progressed in goodness
and service to our fellows. Remembering this long and successful road to wellness,
Rotarians and those that serve require the quality of fortitude You give us.
As we, together with Your grace, have successfully developed answers to pressing
problems, we pray for Your guidance in the eradication of disease and the
concurrent tragedy of the loss of hope we all now face.
Please be with those that suffer and offer them the strength to persevere through
their affliction and pain.
As we pray for those in jeopardy of disease, may we, as Rotarians retain the spirit
to "answer the call" to help.
In thy name we pray, Amen.
America!
Amen.

10. FAMILY

Month of the Family

Let us Pray!

Almighty God, it is appropriate that Rotary's month of the family should occur in the month celebrating the Holy Family and the birth of Your Son. As family's gather and remember their own origins and celebrate who they are as a family unit, we pray they remember those that we help, as Rotarians, in remote places.

We pray that we remember them as our Rotary extended family and wish them the same graces You have given us.

Amen

Family Core

Let us Pray!

Almighty God,

You have given us Family as the core of love in all societies.

May we, as Rotarians, promote family - that all may love their children enough to protect, educate and preserve their family as we do our own. As we take care to preserve our family tradition and instill in our children the values that You have given us, we pray to project to others the closeness and love we give in our own families.

In thy name we pray,

Amen.

Holy Season

Let us Pray!
In this season of great joy we pray for Your guidance in bringing the natural spirit of the Rotarian to as many people in need as possible.
We pray for our immediate families first. Their welfare and happiness are rooted in Your love and our love for them.
As we continue our efforts in so many enterprises we pray that we may not lose track of Rotarian efforts because of the more pressing needs of our families.

We pray to consider others as an extension of family.
Amen.

Legacy

Let us Pray!
We praise You, O Lord, and glorify You for generously providing us with our families.
We pray all to enjoy the enduring legacy of family that You give us in this season of peace and true joy - the basis of all that matters to us.
We pray that our joy and thanksgiving may spread to everyone and their families and that they may recognize You as their source of all that is good and true.
As we come together as a Rotarian family to enjoy this season, instill in us Your love and fellowship.
In grateful appreciation and Thanksgiving we pray!
Amen.

Legacy

Let us pray;
Almighty God, heavenly father we reflect on the precious gifts You have
given us and resolve to protect and preserve the family.
Rotarians will promote the structure You have given us in our Rotary
family with programs that develop future generations of leaders that
extend proven traditions.
All that is good is handed down to us by the passage of family with parents
providing their knowledge and Your goodness.
We pray that we may be as generous in passing on the joy and fulfillment
of all that we find in Rotary.
Amen.

Travel

Let us Pray!
Almighty God, by Your Grace we pray for the safety and protection of all
as they travel and gather with family and friends.
Though journey's may be long and sometimes tedious, we pray for the
great joy of reunion for all.
We pray for the unity of families knowing that the greatest gift we can give
to others is unity and reunion with You.
Amen

Daily Trials

Let us Pray!
May we never forget Your goodness in helping us to provide for our families.
As we face our daily trials in this sweet land of liberty let us recall, each day, the
overwhelming trials of other families in a world that does not have liberty, or, the
ability to grow in the same kind of peace and prosperity we enjoy.
Since Rotary gives us the ability to help those less fortunate, may we project the
values You have given us as Americans, with the same joy we have in our
own families.
In Your name we pray!
Amen.

Holy Season

Let us Pray!
We praise You, O Lord, and glorify You for generously providing us with our families.
We pray all to enjoy the enduring legacy of family You give us in this season of peace and
true joy - the basis of all that matters to us.
We pray that our joy and thanksgiving may spread to everyone and their families and that
they may recognize You as their source of all that is good and true.
As we come together as a Rotarian family to enjoy this season, instill in us Your love and
fellowship -remembering all that You have given us.
In thy name we pray!
Amen.

Rotary Family

Let us Pray!
Almighty God, as Rotarians take action locally and globally each day, we ask Your guidance for our members as we pour our passion, integrity, and intelligence into completing projects that have a lasting impact.
We pray to persevere until we deliver real, lasting solutions as we bridge cultures and connect continents to champion peace, fight illiteracy and poverty, promote clean water and sanitation, and fight disease.
In Thy name we pray,
Amen.

Rotary as Relationships

Let us Pray!
Oh Lord, we praise you and thank you for giving us the relationships we have through Rotary.
We know that we can only do so much for others by ourselves.
We understand that by combining our Rotary relationships here on Marco Island, that we can provide much more for those in need.
With our District and International relationships we can greatly increase our efforts for a world in great need.
We thank You for the blessing of the sum of our efforts in defining common goals and reaching out to others.
We pray that with Your help, our combined relationships can impact: elimination of disease, provide clean water and nutrition, promote education and advance the nobility of Your people.
Amen.

Rotary Spirit

Let us Pray!
In this season of great joy we pray for Your guidance in bringing the
natural spirit of the Rotarian to as many people in need as possible.
We pray for our immediate families first. Their welfare and happiness are
rooted in Your love and our love for them.
As we continue our efforts in so many enterprises we pray that we may
not lose track of Rotarian efforts because of the more pressing needs of
our families.
We pray to consider others as an extension of family.
Amen.

Rotary Unity

From Sunrise Rotary meeting of 4/13/21 and District Conference of 4/17/21

Let us pray,
Almighty God:
You have taught us that: "a house divided against itself cannot stand".
As we see in our time an effort for the division of societal components, we
understand that we cannot seek peace if we make war with each other. We
pray You give us the strength to avoid anything that brings discord.
Bind us closely, as Paul Harris and his associates designed Rotary. May we
remain instruments of Unity in a world torn by differences.
May our Unity of body, mind and spirit, of one heart and soul,
remain with ourselves, our club and Rotary with an attitude born of charity.
We seek to be better as we imitate Your love for us, even if we see no response.
By Your grace, the great Rotary tree of hope, united in charity, with our faith
in You our good God, we pray to enjoy good health of spirit.
With patience and forbearance for others and an understanding of their
needs, we pray to overcome all barriers and differences whether they be:
social, economic, racial or cultural.
Charity, like music for the soul, unites us.
In thy name we pray.
Amen.

11. FOUNDATION

Polio Plus

Let us Pray;

Almighty God, You are our refuge. You are our strength!

By Your grace, we are thankful for Your giving mankind the intelligence and will to develop systems to assemble without personal

contact - which we dearly miss.

By our Covenant with You, our God, You have given us the mission that we will be your people with instruction to serve the "least of these our brethren".

We, as Rotarians, act with solidarity, and, with this strength, You give us greater power to serve others.

As with the great Rotary effort to eradicate Polio, we accept the current crisis as only a deviation from that mission and accept the additional calling.

Our Rotarian prayer is that, with this current crisis, Your Suffering Servants are inspired to holiness in Your kingdom here on Earth as we hope to enter Your kingdom in Heaven.

The Polio **Plus** rallying cry is our call to action and a way for Rotarians to serve You better and more completely.

Guide us with Your grace.

In Thy name we pray,

Amen.

Gift of Life

Let us Pray!

Almighty God, we pray for the success for our fundraising in its many forms and tonight for the need to help children in need and help them to receive Your: "Gift of Life" in its fullest measure.

We understand that our caring for others in need, requires funding from many. We pray our energies for those in need be maximized by enlisting the aid of non-Rotarians.

We pray for Your guidance in directing our efforts for others and that we are ever mindful of their plight.

We pray that our combined Rotary energy always reflect the welfare of the recipient.

Amen.

Will

Let us Pray!
Lord, You are the one who gives us "The Gift of Life."
The Rotary principal of giving is who we are and this comes from You as we continue Your work.
We applaud the dedication and hard work of those that give of themselves to restoring health and a normal life for a child.
Those who receive are the least of Your people, but the best of us because they are our future.
As we use our God given abilities of heart, mind and intellect to help others we pray to use our **will** to comfort and heal the little ones in our world.
The satisfaction we receive, we pray, will propel us to do more.
In Thy name we pray,
Amen!

Cardinal Virtues

Let Us Pray;
As Rotarians, we are thankful for the gifts you have given us for ourselves and our families that we may pass on to those in need:
The gift of the memory of those that have gone before us,
The gift of health and the energy and heart to help others,
The gift of intellect and knowledge thru education and experience,
The gift of will and the drive to persist in our efforts,
The gift of discernment that we may prioritize our efforts, and
The gift of the soul given us in Your word.
Amen.

Assistance for the Basics

Let us pray!
As we make our way through this life we sometimes need to be awakened from our
own problems to finally realize that we long to see your face and are not alone.
As we are accustomed to our comfortable life in paradise, there are others, Rotarians
work to reach, that require assistance for the very basics in life.
As we practice to understand their plight we ask for Your guidance and grace to truly
understand their needs.
We pray that Rotarians work in harmony that we may assist those in need.
In thy name we pray!
Amen

Grace

Let us pray!
In times of tragedy we turn to You, O Lord. Bathe us in Your Grace and consolation.
Give us the gifts of prudence and temperance that we may make the best decisions for
the well being of ourselves and others.
As You inspire all Rotarians to fulfill our humanitarian programs, we pray that our
unity and sense of purpose become the magnet for all in the world that You
desire for us.
In Thy name we pray!
Amen.

Service Above Self

Let us Pray;
O Lord, You have given us the ability to discern, first, what is important to
You in our daily lives.
We have accepted Rotary as the vehicle before us that fulfills Your desire
for us to perform charitable giving on a local and in a worldwide effort.
As Rotarians, we understand our small part in combining with others to
faithfully execute our and Your duties.
We have pledged, by the four way test, to Service Above Self with diligence
and fidelity to Your Word.
Amen.

Spared by Grace

Let us pray!
Almighty God, heavenly father we are extremely thankful for the grace
You have bestowed on us. We are thankful that the extreme destruction of
our precious island did not occur.
We are thankful for the inspiration and dedication of those who respond
with necessary services.
As we adjust to the calamities our community has experienced, we pray
for Your continued grace as we recover.
We pray to remember those less fortunate to bring their lives back to
normal. The struggle they pursue is perhaps more severe than our own.
We pray that the giving nature of Rotarians in our community remain an
inspiration to all.
In thy name we pray!
Amen.

Gifts

Let Us Pray!
As Rotarians, we are thankful for the gifts you have given us for ourselves
and our families that we may pass on to those in need:
The gift of the memory of those that have gone before us,
The gift of health and the energy and heart to help others,
The gift of intellect and knowledge thru education and experience,
The gift of will and the drive to persist in our efforts,
The gift of discernment that we may prioritize our efforts, and
The gift of the soul given us in Your word.
Amen.

Joy of Giving

Let us Pray!
To give anonymously is the greatest satisfaction.
As You, our Lord guides us through our everyday lives, we pray to be,
meekly, last - that we may be first in Your kingdom.
By Rotarians serving others before self, we pray to maintain humility in
giving of our time, talent and treasure.
The true joy we receive - is the only reward we seek.
In thy name we pray,
Amen.

12. FUND RAISING

Joy to Perform

Let us Pray!
Almighty God, as we embark on our most favored and productive means
of raising funds for our Club's projects and programs, we ask that You
give us the joy to perform this most necessary work.
We pray that we may display Your presence in us to others and to take the
opportunity to discuss Rotary.
By invitation to join our club, we understand that we can enhance our
membership as we enhance our programs and projects.
In Thy name we pray,
Amen.

Aid from Non-Rotarians

Let us Pray!
Almighty God, we pray for the success for our fundraising in its many forms.
We understand that our caring for others in need, requires funding from many.
We pray our energies for those in need be maximized by enlisting the aid of non-
Rotarians.
We pray for Your guidance in directing our efforts for others and that we are ever
mindful of their plight.
We pray that our combined Rotary energy always reflect the welfare of the
recipient.
Amen.

Gift of Life
Fundraising

Let us Pray!

Almighty God, we pray for the success for our fundraising in its many forms and tonight for the need to help children in need and help them to receive Your: "Gift of Life" in its fullest measure.

May the little ones in our care be healed and reach maturity to extend generations of productive servants for You, our God.

We understand that our caring for others in need, requires funding from many. We pray our energies for those in need, be maximized by enlisting the aid of non-Rotarians.

We pray for Your guidance in directing our efforts for others and that we are ever mindful of their plight.

We pray that our combined Rotary energy always reflect the welfare of the recipient, especially the least of these, our children.

Amen.

Season of Hope

Let us pray,

Almighty God, by your grace You have given us the Gift of Life.

In this season of hope, let us suffer the little children. They know not where the pain, lack of energy and necessary extra care comes from. They see their playmates at play that they cannot take part in. They need more sleep, cannot engage in school as their playmates do. They naturally trust in their parents and others to help them. To give them hope and energy to play and learn.

We have seen how frail and fragile our life is based on current events.

We seem to be reminded every so often.

We pray, Oh God for our own energy and dedication to give the Gift of Life, a gift of a future and a gift for children in need of heart repair that they may produce future generations of Your people in awe and dedication to You with hope for Your world.

In our human frailty we pray to sustain the life You have given these - Your children.

You have empowered Rotarians to give strength to the vulnerable, hope to their hearts.

In thy name we pray,

Amen.

Grace

Let us Pray!

Almighty God, we thank you and praise You for looking over our projects
and fundraising. Our efforts would not be successful without the grace
You provide.

We pray that those we try to help may be blessed to make progress in their
lives and give back to others as we have tried to give to them.

May the spirit of Rotary be Your spirit and, inspired by You, we can help
all others we come in contact with.

In Thy name we pray.

Amen.

13. GRACE

Pastoral Virtues

Let Us Pray!
O Lord, in our daily application of the Four Way Test, grant us:
The virtues of **patience** to **prudently** discern others points-of-view,
Temperance to thoughtfully explain our position, and
To impart **justice** with the **fortitude** Your grace gives us.
Grant us the vision of **Faith**,
The inspiration of **Hope**, and
The blessings of **Charity**.
Amen.

Personal Gifts

Let Us Pray!
As Rotarians, we are thankful for the gifts you have given us for ourselves
and our families that we may pass on to those less fortunate:
The gift of the memory of those that have gone before us,
The gift of health and the energy and heart to help others,
The gift of intellect and knowledge thru education and experience,
The gift of will and the drive to persist in our efforts,
The gift of discernment that we may prioritize our efforts, and
The gift of the soul given us in Your word.
Amen.

Joy of Giving

Let us Pray!

To give anonymously is the greatest satisfaction.

As You, our Lord guides us through our everyday lives, we pray to be,
meekly, last - that we may be first in Your kingdom.

By Rotarians serving others before self, we pray to maintain humility in
giving of our time, talent and treasure.

The true joy we receive - is the only reward we seek.

Amen.

Your Word

Let us Pray:

As we live with Rotary, help us to hear Your Word. Live Your Word. Speak Your
Word. Impart Your Word.

Help us to keep Your Word alive, when it is drowned out by Your enemies.

Let us feel Your Courage when we are down.

Fill us with Your Strength when we are weak.

Give us the Grace to remain dignified when we feel oppressed by some with
opposing points of view - that Rotary may prevail for remaining loyal to Your
Most Holy Will.

Amen.

Life

Let us pray,

Almighty God,

We, Your people, are engulfed in great tragedy and trial.

There are those far away that are looking for hope of survival as we lay
secure in relative safety.

Our collective prayer is for their welfare and safety.

We know not life in harm's way.

We do not live in

the privation, desolation and lack of security they experience.

Evil and oppression surround them directly at every moment without regard for
human life. They feel only the weight of subjugation and eventual death.

We ask that You, our God, to purge the fear, anxiety, frustration and sense of
abandonment they now experience.

We pray especially for the women and all children in harms way.

We ask Your intercession to rescue those that are at risk for survival and are at the
disposal of these unnatural events.

For those that are actively involved in rescue efforts we pray that their training
and expertise may give them the will, motivation and dedication to persevere and
insure safety and a life that You promise.

As You have done so often, we pray You convert evil and oppression without
their sacrifice.

As Rotarians, may we envelope Your ideals in prayer that the prayer for peace
may envelope all.

In Thy name we pray!

Amen.

14. HEALTH

Cardinal Virtues

Let Us Pray!
As Rotarians, we are thankful for the gifts you have given us for ourselves
and our families that we may pass on to those in need:
The gift of the memory of those that have gone before us,
The gift of health and the energy and heart to help others,
The gift of intellect and knowledge thru education and experience,
The gift of will and the drive to persist in our efforts,
The gift of discernment that we may prioritize our efforts, and
The gift of the soul given us in Your word.
Amen.

Cognitive Impairment

Let us Pray!
We pray for those in our midst that may be degenerating in mind and body. We pray that
they may be at peace with You and the world around them.
We recognize that our thoughtfulness and attention to others is a cornerstone of Rotary.
We ask You to keep us ever mindful of their contribution to our families and to society.
May we recognize always their experience and attention to us and others in their long
and productive lives, and pray that their spirit
be passed on to us by Your grace.
Amen

Decline

Let us Pray!

Almighty God and father of all, as Rotarians we continue to experience the decline of our loved ones.

We do pray for their recovery and realize their slow departure from us and their welcome by You.

We pray for those that see to their welfare and show with loving care respect as they share in their memories together.

As a family of Rotarians, we pray to share with the caregivers among us their loving experience.

In Thy name we pray,

Amen.

Fundraising

Let Us Pray!

We are motivated to be Rotarians and work towards Rotary principals.

Since we are also motivated by Your will, we pray that our Rotary efforts can fulfill our deepest longing to please You.

We know that each Rotary project, each fundraising is difficult to fully complete by most of us.

We pray that our time, our health and the health of our loved ones, will allow us the motivation to be good Rotarians, in terms of service, to our club and the community.

We pray that our priorities recognize Rotary as part of who we are with our time, our treasure and talent.

Amen.

Freedom

Let us pray,
Almighty God, as You bless America with Your unbounded grace, we
pray all to take the renewed freedom we are experiencing seriously.
Rotarians understand that we are blessed to share our gifts with gratitude
and a spirit of respect for others health and well being.
As we gradually progress to total freedom of movement and affiliation
with others, we ask to never forget the tragedy that many others have
endured during the worst of times.
As professionals work to provide cures for illness, we pray all to
understand these difficult times as prologue to a world of peace and
dedication to improved health and wellness.
In thy name we pray,
Amen.

Overcoming Distance

Let us pray;
Almighty God, as we experience distance between us and our fellow
Rotarians we rely on You to give us the strength to carry forward our goals
for our family, friends and for Rotary.
In all trying times, our respect for each other lets us use the guidelines You
have given us to provide "Service above Self".
Respect is critical to our fight. It is essential to turning the tide against our
common health enemy. There is no path out of this test of Rotary
dedication and will on our own. Without Your guidance our efforts
cannot succeed.
By Your grace we pray You protect those that, by their choice, are engaged
in nursing our way ahead in gratitude.
In thy name we pray,
Amen.

Inoculation

Let is Pray;
A major area of focus for us, as Rotarians, is Disease Prevention and Treatment.
As daunting as this goal may be, we ask You to bless us in our efforts to do all that
we, a small group of participants, can dedicate ourselves to.
We pray that those areas of the world that are closed off to inoculation and
education will respond to Your will and submit to our help.
As we make progress in Your name please help all Rotarians to persevere in our
quest to improve others health.
In thy name we pray,
Amen.

Fortitude

Let us Pray;
If not for You, Almighty God, mankind could not have progressed in
goodness and service to our fellows. Remembering this long and
successful road to wellness, Rotarians and those that serve require the
quality of fortitude You give us.
As we, together with Your grace, have successfully developed answers to
pressing problems, we pray for Your guidance in the eradication of disease
and the concurrent tragedy of the loss of hope we all now face.
Please be with those that suffer and offer them the strength to persevere
through their affliction and pain.
As we pray for those in jeopardy of disease, may we, as Rotarians retain
the spirit to "answer the call" to help.
In thy name we pray,
Amen.

With a Suffering Spirit

Let us Pray:
As children of God and Rotarians we are well aware and thankful for our health
and well being as we enjoy this beautiful place.
We are aware that some of us, and those close to us, do suffer from ailments and
deteriorating health.
We pray that your Spirit will encircle them and provide them with the
comfort they need.
Help them to realize, as well, that their club is with them in their time of trial.
Amen.

Prayer for Missing Rotarians

Let us Pray!
We pray, o Lord, for Your continued consideration of those members of our
Rotary Club that cannot be with us for health reasons;
Roy Birkland for the care of his wife Pat.
Ralph Lalli for the care of his wife Lorraine.
Pam Michel and Dottie Weiner.
As loyal Rotarians they have given of themselves for many years and we pray that
we may be ever mindful of that commitment.

As we progress together with You in Your work, O Lord, we pray that You
continue to guide us all in our efforts and in the care of our families.
Amen.

Use of Time, Talent and Treasure

Let Us Pray!

We are pleased to be motivated by You to work toward Rotary principals.

We pray that our time, our health and the health of our loved ones, will allow us to be good Rotarians, in terms of service, to our club and the community.

For those who receive our service, we wish Your continued presence in their lives for their support and comfort.

We pray that our priorities recognize Rotary as part of who we are with our time, our treasure and talent.

Amen.

Comfort

Let us Pray:

As children of God and Rotarians we are well aware and thankful for our health and well being as we enjoy this beautiful place.

We are aware that some of us, and those close to us, do suffer from ailments and deteriorating health.

We pray that your Spirit will encircle them and provide them with the comfort they need.

Help them to realize, as well, that their club is with them in their time of trial.

Amen.

Cancer

Let us Pray!

Almighty God

We praise you and thank you for preserving the health of those here present and pray that you attend to the health of those we hold dear to us.

All of us have been touched in some way by the scourge of Cancer and understand the scourging of your Son, Jesus and the profound nature of His suffering.

We, with Your help, have achieved some measure of success preserving the lives of those afflicted with this dreaded evil.

We take courage from examples of those who have survived and ask for your guidance to all that are involved in research and care of Cancer victims.

Thru thy name we pray.

Amen

Let us Pray!

Cancer

Let us pray;

Almighty God

We praise you and thank you for preserving the health of those here present and pray that you attend to the health of those we hold dear to us.

All of us have been touched in some way by the scourge of Cancer and understand the sadness and frustration of those suffering, their loved ones and those that care for them.

We, Your people and with Your help, have achieved some measure of success preserving the lives of those afflicted with this dreaded evil.

We take courage from examples of those who have survived and those that have been in remission. We ask for your guidance to all that are involved in research and those that care of Cancer victims.

Thru thy name we pray.

Amen

Self Health

Let us Pray!
O God, we are in awe of Your insight and guidance as Rotarians. We are obliged to be aware of our own health and personal well being as much as we are concerned with others welfare.
We understand that without our own ability to perform the tasks that are before us, we cannot fulfill Your will and be of benefit to others and their needs.
We thank You for the talents and expertise of all who administer to us and to all those that we cherish, in order that we may perform Your service to others.
In thy name we pray,
Amen.

Local Providers

Let is Pray;
As Rotarians focus on Disease Prevention and Treatment, we pray for Your guidance of our local providers.
Please guide them in their education, analysis and treatment of those in our community who need their skills, dedication and care.
As we make progress in Your name, please help all Rotarians to persevere in our quest to improve others health.
In thy name we pray,
Amen!

Priorities

Let Us Pray!

We are motivated to be Rotarians and work towards Rotary principals.
Since we are also motivated by Your will, we pray that our Rotary efforts
can fulfill our deepest longing to please You.

We know that each Rotary project, each fundraising is difficult to fully
complete by most of us.

We pray that our time, our health and the health of our loved ones, will
allow us the motivation to be good Rotarians, in terms of service, to our
club and the community.

We pray that our priorities recognize Rotary as part of who we are with
our time, our treasure and talent.

Amen.

Healing

Let us pray!

Almighty God, heavenly father we are obliged as Rotarians and as Your
children to engage and assist those that are less fortunate than ourselves.
Especially our children.

Rotarians are committed to helping children and families worldwide by
eliminating the burden of disease and deformities in order to give them a
life of joy and fulfillment.

We pray that You guide us in helping those that program assistance and
care - to give all a fair chance at the life You have planned for us.

With the complications of facilitating missions, counseling, collaboration,
and education - the mission is daunting. With Your counseling and grace
we pray that all may be healed to live productive lives.

In Thy name we pray,

Amen.

Children

Let us Pray;
Almighty God, we thank You and pray to You for the health and safety of
our children.
As Rotarians continue to give to causes to improve the lives of those
generations following, we ask for Your blessing on their efforts for self
development. We also ask that You continue to protect them in
development of a health body, mind and spirit.
Rotarians continue to provide scholarships for their education. Rotarians
seek to improve children's health by eliminating disease and create good
health habits. We turn to You to instill in our children the spirit to develop
Rotarian values and then pass on this Your will, for all.
Our cause is Your cause. Give us the will to sacrifice what is necessary in
the development of future generations.
In thy name we pray,
Amen.

Motivation

Let Us Pray!
We are motivated to be Rotarians and work towards Rotary principals.
Since we are also motivated by Your will, we pray that our Rotary efforts
can fulfill our deepest longing to please You.
We know that each Rotary project, each fundraising is difficult to fully
complete by most of us.
We pray that our time, our health and the health of our loved ones, will
allow us the motivation to be good Rotarians, in terms of service, to our
club and the community.
We pray that our priorities recognize Rotary as part of who we are with
our time, our treasure and talent.
Amen.

Health and Welfare

Let us pray!
Almighty God, heavenly father we pray for the health and welfare of our children.
We pray that all parents take the responsibility and be inspired with the love and
faith You have given us to dedicate to future generations.
We pray that caregivers, teachers and child advocates nurture and protect
those in their care.
We pray that children may develop childhood memories making them good
citizens and, as Your children, that they project that image to future generations.
In thy name we pray!
Amen.

In Rotary Service

Let us pray;
Almighty God, as we come together today to contemplate our personal
well being, we pray to You to help us to understand and dedicate our
health efforts as protecting the life You have given us.
We understand that when we are in good health we are better able to serve
You as Rotarians.
We pray for strength in our bodies, our hearts and our minds: that our
memory, our intellect and our souls may act in purity and dedication to
the love of others.
In this coming year we pray that Rotary success is a reflection of all that
You have given us.
In thy name we pray,
Amen.

Hero's Song

Let us pray;

Songs are sung of hero's past, of those distinguished in battle, or elevated to great position.

But what of the great mass of mankind who, by God's grace, performed with valor, honor and without the glory of worldly recognition.

Those that did what had to be done in their time and in a way that gives glory to God: unselfish and tempered by their time. Those unsung.

They live today, in a different way, a different place, as warriors in public service and are spontaneous in doing right in a time of crisis.

They have learned to do right sometimes by how they were brought up and then through training. They live among us.

Respect and honor. Unselfish. Hero's are not to be worshiped, they do not care to be worshiped. If ego exists in the hero, question whether they are hero's?

Duty, honor, country, community.

The live where dedication to duty is distinctive and valor is common.

Where their working realm is a zone apart, not to be pierced by outside thought.

The hero mocks the self proclaimed by his humility, his simple act of not reacting in his own self interest. He does not proclaim he is the greatest, the best. Those that are self adorned.

His cause is not himself.

The hero does and walks away. He hides in the comfort of duty performed.

In thy name we pray,

Amen.

15. HOLIDAYS

Christmas

Let us Pray!
Oh God of eternal grace, we take Your Holy Family as our example this week.
We pray for Your guidance to model our own families after Your Holy Family.
As we honor the birth of the Prince of Peace we ask for Your grace, as Rotarians,
to promote peace through understanding and our own good work, in order to
protect and preserve families throughout a troubled world.
By Your grace.
Amen.

Christmas

Let us Pray;
Lord, as we celebrate the birth of our lord and savior, we pray to follow his
word and the word of our motto:
"Service above Self".
As You gave Your son to us, we pray to continue collectively to present
those principles to others and project them with the joy that comes
through to the love you have given to us.
As we translate Your love into charity and giving in this season, we pray
that others will join us to keep You in Christmas.
Amen.

Christmas and Legacy

Let us Pray:
As we prepare for the celebration of the birth of our savior we pray to
remember our legacy and goals as Rotarians.
We can change the world with the pressure of Your love that we give to
all. We understand that it does require our inginuity and creativity. These
are gifts that You have given us. Through our own perseverance and the
gift of Your grace we pray to endure understanding that the final result
enhances Your will be done.
In thy name we pray,
Amen.

Rotary Family

Let us Pray!
We praise You, O Lord, and glorify You for generously providing us with our families.
We pray all to enjoy the enduring legacy of family You give us in this season of peace and
true joy - the basis of all that matters to us.
We pray that our joy and thanksgiving may spread to everyone and their families and that
they may recognize You as their source of all that is good and true.
As we come together as a Rotarian family to enjoy this season, instill in us Your love and
fellowship -remembering all that You have given us.
In thy name we pray!
Amen.

Peace on Earth

Let us pray:
Almighty God, heavenly father
We reflect on the birth of a child in this season of hope, and pray for "peace on earth goodwill to men".
As Rotarians, we follow the Rotary action plan for peace on earth. We pray to you for guidance that we may follow this plan for our service to those less fortunate.
Almighty God, you have empowered us with intelligence and the will to achieve Your goals. As we embrace this Rotary area of focus and tradition, we pray for success in achieving the Peace and Conflict Resolution promised to us by You in sacred scripture.
Guide us to reach out to others, to take action, to become involved in meaningful plans to improve the lives of others.
We pray for the peace of this season to overwhelm us that we may positively influence others to work with us and bring "peace on earth" to all mankind.
In thy name we pray,
Amen.

Holy Week 4/7/20

Let us pray,
Almighty God, In our isolation Rotarians understand that we are not isolated from You in this Holy Week.
Through Your grace we pledge that we, in at least a small way, find ways to connect with the lost, the lonely and the forgotten in this crisis in order to "serve the least of these —-".
Give us the devotion, strength and discipline to project a positive attitude in these uncertain times.
We are brought to common communication to others thru You and we work as Rotarians in communion with you.
No one knows but You what the future holds and we except that the future is in Your hands..
We pray that You Bless the faithfully departed and we look forward to a new world in Your image after this time of our trial.
In thy name we pray,
Amen.

Month of the Family

Let us Pray!

Almighty God, it is appropriate that Rotary's month of the family should occur in the month celebrating the Holy Family and the birth of Your Son. As family's gather and remember their own origins and celebrate who they are as a family unit, we pray they remember those that we help, as Rotarians, in remote places.

We pray that we remember them as our Rotary extended family and wish them the same graces You have given us.

Amen.

Family

Let us Pray!

Oh God of eternal grace, we take Your Holy Family as our example this week. We pray for Your guidance to model our own families after Your Holy Family. As we honor the birth of the Prince of Peace we ask for Your grace, as Rotarians, to promote peace through understanding and our own good work, in order to protect and preserve families throughout a troubled world.

By Your grace.

Amen.

Good Counsel

Let us pray!
As You come into our hearts in this giving season, we pray that we be willing to
absorb Your Good Counsel, and think of You first with empathy for all.
Understanding that You measure Rotarians by the charge You have given us, by Your
grace, we pledge to thoughtfully apply Rotary principals because they are Your
principals. Help us to grow Rotary by implementing Your will.
In this season of hope for all, may we share with all and manifest the destiny of love
and caring for those who otherwise might not enjoy the gifts You have given us.
In thy name we pray!
Amen.

Election Day

Let us Pray,
Almighty God, we praise You and thank You for providing us with this
wonderful world and beautiful community.
We pray for Your grace in protecting our citizens that they may be guided
by our elected officials. Always knowing that You have provided us with
life, liberty and the pursuit of happiness.
Our environment is a gift from You, and we pray for official guidance in
the protection of what we have that inspires us to be part of this
community.
In Thy name we pray,
Amen.

Election Day

Let us Pray:

As we take the responsibility to preserve, protect and defend the great land You have allowed us to live in we pray that You be with us as we choose those to represent us for a fair and just system of government.

We pray that those we elect will think of the people and their welfare first and foremost that we may all prosper in this great land of freedom and liberty.

May all participants remember:

Is it the truth

Is it fair to all concerned

Will it build goodwill and better friendships, and

Is it beneficial to all concerned

In thy name we pray,

Amen

Family

Let us Pray!

We praise You, O Lord, and glorify You for generously providing is with our families.

We pray all to enjoy the enduring legacy of family that You give us in this season of peace and true joy - the basis of all that matters to us.

We pray that our joy and thanksgiving may spread to everyone and their families and that they may recognize You as their source of all that is good and true.

As we come together as a Rotarian family to enjoy this season, instill in us Your love and fellowship.

In grateful appreciation and Thanksgiving we pray!

Amen.

Flag Day

Let us pray;

Almighty God, Heavenly Father,

You have blessed us by giving us a country of diverse people and opportunities.

We look to our flag, the Stars and Stripes, as the symbol of this blessed land to be cherished and protected.

We look to your history and the sacrifices you resemble.

We thank You for the giving hearts and minds of those who have gone before us protecting our Banner of Freedom and Liberty.

We see in you the dreams and hopes for our home-the United States of America.

As our standard is raised throughout the world, we pray it portrays our nation to all as the highest standard of Faith, Hope and Love, and builds goodwill and better friendships - beneficial to all.

In thy name we pray,

Amen.

Hanakkah

Let us pray:

Almighty God, As we enter the Holy Season, we pray the prayer of the Jewish celebration of the Festival of Lights:

"Our God, Ruler of the Universe, who makes us holy through Your commandments, and commands us to light the Hanukkah lights."

We join together as Rotarians to commemorate and rededicate our common love of You, our God by working for freedom from oppression as we work for freedom of religious expression.

We pray to eliminate our differences because Rotarians recognize that this is a season of light, illuminating our common desire for unity with You, our God.

In thy name we pray,

Amen.

Holy Days

Let us Pray!

Almighty God,

As Rotarians, we are pledged to understand, respect and dignify religious preferences. We do this with Your guidance and grace as we celebrate these holy times with each other.

Our feeling for our salvation and living with You, now and in the future, is our goal. As our faiths merge and coincide in service to You, we pray that they re-merge in service to others.

Rotarians transcend national boundaries, cultures and religious orientation as a way of performing Your will that we may serve "the least of these" in their need.

We pray to continue in this great joy of giving with Your inspiration in this Holy time.

In thy name we pray!

Amen.

Holy Week

Let us Pray;

Almighty God, in this holy week, we pray for the salvation of all mankind. As Rotarians, may we continue to extend our goodwill, in Your name, to our friends here at our host club by our participation in their programs.

We pray for Your guidance home, and that we may return to our home clubs enriched by our friends here and pass their greetings and goodwill to all.

Amen.

Holy Season

Let us pray!
We ask You to continue to pour Your grace on Rotarians as we proceed in our programs promoting world peace.
During this Holy Season we pray that all may see the value of others.
Especially their adversaries.
The standards You have set for Your people are high considering our human frailty.
As we place You above all others, we ask that all may be joined together in Your name as the spirit of this season comes into our hearts.
Amen.

Holy Season

Let us pray;
Almighty God,
Our feeling for our salvation and living with You, now and in the future, is our goal. As our faiths merge and coincide in service to You, we pray that they re-emerge in service to others.
Rotarians transcend national boundaries, cultures and religious orientation as a way of performing Your will that we may serve "the least of these" in their need.
We pray to continue in this great joy of giving with Your inspiration in this Holy time.
In thy name we pray!
Amen.

Independence Day

God, Bless America
We are a land of <u>Your</u> people. We pray, thankfully, for the grace you bestow on our nation.
Land that I love;
We are in awe and appreciation deep in our hearts for Your creation.
Stand beside her,
Thru our faults, our disunity, our pride
And guide her,
We cannot improve America without Your grace
Through the night
The darkness of despair, of anxiety brought on by our own human condition
With the light from above
Your light is the promise of goodness at the end of a tunnel of our own making
From the mountains
Heights which mankind can only achieve with You
To the prairie
A diversified terrain of promise
To the oceans white with foam
With You we have spanned the greatest boundaries provided by our freedom.
God, Bless America
Our Home - blessed by You at our founding
Sweet Home - with goodness and justice for all.
In thy name we pray,
Amen.

Independence Day and Change of Leadership

Let us pray!
As we celebrate our nations independence we recall that we are
"One Nation Under God".
We recall all of the benefits You have given us as we are able to pursue life,
liberty and happiness.
We pray our Representative Republic always remembers why freedom is so important.
As Rotarians, we have the freedom to choose those we wish to help and pray Your grace
permits us to choose wisely.
As the "torch is passed" and our new Board takes effect, we pray that Rotary generosity
continues this year in its dedication to our areas of focus: to build international
relationships, improve lives, and create a better world to support our peace
efforts and end polio forever.
We pray for Your guidance as Rotarians project these American values for others.
In Thy name we pray!
Amen.

Service Members
4th of July, Memorial Day, Independence Day

Let us Pray;

O Lord, we pray first for Your guidance in the preservation of our nation as we exercise the freedom you have given us for our life, liberty and pursuit of happiness.

For those that have sacrificed so much to give us this franchise, we pray they may be remembered by all for the unselfish dedication we can only hope to emulate as Rotarians. We pray for those left behind at home, that they may be secure in the knowledge that a grateful nation is with them in their prayers for the safe return of their loved ones.

Almighty God, protect and guide us to consider Your will be done.

Amen.

Memorial Day

Let us Pray!

Almighty God, this nation thrives because of the service of our Armed Forces Veterans. Their sacrifices have protected our freedoms, our families and our America.

We pray that this nation continue to respect and support what veterans have won in battle against continued evolving evil.

We pray You heal those that suffer from their sacrifice.

We ask that You comfort those left behind while they defend us.

For the families of those lost, may they know, that Rotarians support and love them as they grieve their loss.

As Rotarians pursue Peace and Conflict Resolution,

we pray for the time of judgement when: "One nation shall not raise the sword against another, nor shall they train for war again".

In thy name we pray,

Amen.

Your Will be Done

Let us Pray;

O Lord, we pray first for Your guidance in the preservation of our nation
as we exercise the freedom you have given us for our life, liberty and
pursuit of happiness.

For those that have sacrificed so much to give us this franchise, we pray
they may be remembered by all for the unselfish dedication we can only
hope to emulate as Rotarians.

We pray for those left behind at home, that they may be secure in the
knowledge that a grateful nation is with them in their prayers for the safe
return of their loved ones.

Almighty God, protect and guide us to consider Your will be done.

Amen.

Memorial Day

Let us pray,

As we picture the acres of bright white headstones spanning the landscape
of our memories, let us imagine each one draped in our flag of freedom.
For those that have given their lives for our freedoms, we pause to reflect
on the shock, sorrow and grief of the parents, the wives, children and
loved ones when they learned that their warrior for freedom would no
longer be with them in person. Their grief is our own grief.

We pray to keep those who made the ultimate sacrifice alive in our
memory, and mourn with the those that were closest to them.

"A greater love hath no one than to lay down their life for a friend". But to
lay down their life for people they do not know individually, but only
knowing that they are Americans, deserves a special place in Your
Heavenly home.

In the name of those lost, we pray that their spirit live on with us, and to
paraphrase Chief Joseph of the Nez Perce Indian tribe, that someday:
"may we fight no more forever."

In thy name we pray,

Amen.

Memorial Day

Let us Pray!
Oh Lord, who gives Americans the proven courage to give of ourselves
to others, we pray that those who have fallen for our great cause of
liberty, be counted among those in Your Heavenly Kingdom.

O beautiful for heroes proved In liberating strife,
Who more than self their country loved,
And mercy more than life!

O Beautiful for patriot dream
That sees beyond the years
Thine alabaster cities gleam,
Undimmed by human tears!

America! America! God shed Your grace on thee,
And crown their good with brotherhood
From sea to shining sea!
In Thy name we pray,
Amen.

Warriors

Let us Pray!
Almighty God:
Some were born to be warriors.
Some went to grow up.
Some because it was the only job available or, in their innocence, had a romantic
notion of military life.
Whatever there need; they trained, they tired and ached, and grew into a fighting
force of discipline and dedication to protect their nation.
When they joined some had the intention of protecting our liberty and at some point
the rest realized that freedom wasn't free and that they were ordained to
be our protectors.
By Your gracious hand they overcame fear and, with humble valor, the camaraderie
that made our heroes a force became a gift of love You gave them and us.
For the memory of those that gave their lives for us and, for their sacrifice, we are
grateful, Lord, for the inspiration You have given them to "Serve Above Self".
God, continue to bless America!
Amen.

Memorial Day

Let us Pray!
Almighty God, as we pass the one short day of remembering others, we pray
we do not forget the sacrifices that our Armed Forces have made for us.
Our human nature leads us on as we become absorbed in our individual lives.
Please let us take the signal from yesterday and integrate those memories into
what we do every day.
As Rotarians, our longevity as an international group of individuals and clubs
doing good, could only come from Your blessing.
Our good comes from You, and we pray that our small Rotary sacrifices may
be remembered as a gift from those who have given us our freedom
through You.
Amen.

Crusade

Almighty God,
With Your grace we celebrate the anniversary of the success of another
great crusade against evil.
With Your inspiration, the forces of Your good could only succeed in such
a massive effort with Your will for all good people to prevail against evil.
On this anniversary, Rotarians seek to emulate the dedication and sacrifice
of this great part of mankind.
We can only remember the values of courage, bravery and sacrifice taught
to us, that Rotarians in their small way, can help others to enjoy the life
that those of that great crusade have provided for us.
As we pass on the will of those that have sacrificed, and Your will for us
please continue to inspire Rotarians to build good will and greater
friendships of all.
In thy name we pray,
Amen!

Memorial Day

Let us Pray;
O Lord, we pray first for Your guidance in the preservation of our nation as we exercise the freedom you have given us for our life, liberty and pursuit of happiness.
For those that have sacrificed so much to give us this franchise, we pray they may be remembered by all for the unselfish dedication we can only hope to emulate as Rotarians.
We pray for those left behind at home, that they may be secure in the knowledge that a grateful nation is with them in their prayers for the safe return of their loved ones.
Almighty God, protect and guide us to consider Your will be done.
Amen.

New Year

Let us pray
Almighty God, It is that time, at calendar yearend, that we account for the blessings You have given us.
Many of Your people have experienced great trial and tribulation. We take comfort in knowing that You, our God, are there for council and hope.
Thrrough it all You have given us the intellect and drive to persevere and eventually conquer a devastating desease.
As we reflect the true spirit of Rotary in a greater way in life, we ask for Your continued guidance. We pray to reflect on Your will for Your people.
We pray to bring Rotary strength thru unity as we do Your work. Unity is rotary's strength. With dedication, measured reflection and care, as we enter a new calendar year, we ask You to continue to bless Rotarians and our programs, as we adapt, modify our actions and programs to meet new challenges.
In thy name we pray,
Amen.

New Year

Let us pray -
Almighty God, It is that time, at calendar year end, that we account for the
blessings You have given us.
Many of Your people have experienced great trial and tribulation. We take
comfort in knowing that You, our God, are there for council and hope.
Through it all You have given us the intellect and drive to persevere and
eventually conquer a devastating desease.
As we reflect the true spirit of Rotary in a greater way in life, we ask for Your
continued guidance. We pray to reflect on Your will for Your people.
We pray to bring Rotary strength thru unity as we do Your work. Unity is rotary's
strength. With dedication, measured reflection and care, as we enter a new Rotary
year, we ask You to continue to bless Rotarians and our programs, as we adapt,
modify our actions and programs to meet new challenges.
In thy name we pray,
Amen.

New Year

Let us Pray!
Almighty God, we thank You for the many gifts you have given us this year.
The greatest gift we can receive is the hope You give us for a peaceful world. A
world here on earth that is equal to our ultimate gift of heaven.
As we attend our Rotarian duties in the coming year, we pray for Your guidance
to ensure cooperation with others because there needs are not always our needs.
We pray that the best of our mutual efforts be found by working together.
Amen!

Resolve

Let us pray;
Almighty God,
Recent events, which we judge to be both unjustified and unpunished,
cannot perpetuate if our Republic is to continue and thrive on the basis of
"Liberty and Justice for all".
We pray, O Lord, for the resolve to defend America against its dissolution.
We ask for Your intercession in the affairs of all by re-enforcing our hearts
with the fortitude and will desired by our mutual love for each other.
We pray that as Rotarians practice the building of good will, that we build
a contagion of better friendships to heal the destructive practices we see.
We pray for Your grace that our link is the good we do, to create an
infectious chain of good that overcomes the evil we see.
In thy name we pray,
Amen.

Pearl Harbor

Let us pray,
Almighty God, As we recall that day 80 years ago that America was
brutally attacked without warning, our nation lost young people of
principal and dedication.
By Your will, we pray now for vigilance against forces of evil and dedicate
ourselves to serving new generations as our means of strengthening our
nation and community.
To those lost as they honored our country and us, they performed their
Duty with a courage born of the values You have given to all mankind. We
pray, our God, to emulate that courage and valor with our service.
Thru Rotary programs such as RLI, Youth Exchange,
S4TL, training and education, we pray for Your guidance as Rotarians
salute those lost by educating generations succeeding us.
In thy name we pray,
Amen.

Preserving Freedom

Let us Pray;

O Lord, we pray first for Your guidance in the preservation of our nation as we exercise the freedom you have given us for our life, liberty and pursuit of happiness.

For those that have sacrificed so much to give us this franchise, we pray they may be remembered by all for the unselfish dedication we can only hope to emulate as Rotarians.

We pray for those left behind at home, that they may be secure in the knowledge that a grateful nation is with them in their prayers for the safe return of their loved ones.

Almighty God, protect and guide us to consider Your will be done.

Amen.

Transcending Boundaries

Our feeling for our salvation and living with You, now and in the future, is our goal. As our faiths merge and coincide in service to You, we pray that they re-merge in service to others.

Rotarians transcend national boundaries, cultures and religious orientation as a way of performing Your will that we may serve "the least of these" in their need.

We pray to continue in this great joy of giving with Your inspiration in this Holy time.

In thy name we pray!

Amen.

Thanksgiving

Let us Pray!
We praise You, O Lord, and glorify You for generously providing us with our families.
We pray all to enjoy the enduring legacy of family You give us in this season of peace and true joy - the basis of all that matters to us.
We pray that our joy and thanksgiving may spread to everyone and their families and that they may recognize You as their source of all that is good and true.
As we come together as a Rotarian family to enjoy this season, instill in us Your love and fellowship -remembering all that You have given us.
In thy name we pray!
Amen.

Thanksgiving (Best said slowly)

Let Us Pray!
Almighty God, as your bountiful harvest enters our body this
Thanksgiving Day
we pray that you enter also our heart, our mind, our memory, our intellect, our will and our soul
that we may give thanks to You by giving to others.
Amen.

Thanksgiving

Let us pray,
Almighty God, in this season dedicated to our thanksgiving for the
blessing You have given us, we pray for the souls of those faithfully
departed from us and taken into Your eternal home.
As the sum and substance of their being, their soul, has impressed upon us
the goodness that they received in Your grace, we pray for Your guidance
and grace that we may also pass on our soulful memory as a Rotary family.
We pray that this Rotary heritage, these memories of dedication and
success from our past, be translated in energy and resolve that this blessed
season of sacrifice inspires.
In thy name we pray,
Amen

Thanksgiving

Let us Pray;
As we look to our nations past, we are thankful for Your grace in giving
our early settlers the courage and resolve to persevere in a new and harsh
environment.
As we endeavor to emulate their example we pray for Your guidance, as
Rotarians, to fulfill Your will as we give back to others less fortunate.
Lord, give us Your grace to accept what You have given us as a pure gift of
who You are. We pray that our innermost peace be projected to all.
Amen.

Thanksgiving

Let Us Pray!
Almighty God, as we gather with family and friends this Thanksgiving Day, we pray that thru Your bountiful harvest, we remember those that have helped produce our food because they may not be as fortunate as ourselves.
We pray, as Rotarians, that You fill our heart, our mind, our memory, our intellect, our will, and our soul that we may best give thanks to You by giving to others with "Service above Self".
Amen.

Veteran's Day

Let us Pray;
O Lord, we pray first for Your guidance in the preservation of our nation as we exercise the freedom you have given us for our life, liberty and pursuit of happiness.
For those that have sacrificed so much to give us this franchise, we pray they may be remembered by all for the unselfish dedication we can only hope to emulate as Rotarians.
We pray for those left behind at home, that they may be secure in the knowledge that a grateful nation is with them in their prayers for the safe return of their loved ones.
Almighty God, protect and guide us to consider Your will be done.
Amen.

VE Day, VJ Day

Almighty God,

With Your grace we celebrate the anniversary of the success of another
great crusade against evil.

With Your inspiration, the forces of Your good
could only succeed in such a massive effort with Your will for all good
people to prevail against evil.

On this anniversary, Rotarians seek to emulate the dedication and sacrifice
of this great part of mankind.

We can only remember the values of courage, bravery and sacrifice taught
to us, that Rotarians in their small way, can help others to enjoy the life
that those of that great crusade have provided for us.

As we pass on the will of those that have sacrificed, and Your will for us,
please continue to inspire Rotarians to build good will and greater
friendships of all.

In thy name we pray,

Amen!

16. INSTALLATION

Change of Leadership

Let us Pray!
Almighty God, heavenly father, we are here to serve.
We are humbled by the need for help by so many. As a Rotary Club we
have endeavored to discover where we can help and proceeded to
implement programs to assist our fellows.
The heartwarming co-operation and help from all with their time, talent
and treasure propels us all into a new year of hope.
With faith in You, and hope that we can project whatever we have to
others, and the charity built into the human soul by You, our God, we
pray for Your guidance and care moving forward into a new Rotary year.
In thy name we pray,
Amen

Installation Dinner

Let Us Pray!
We are joined here together in Your name to transfer our clubs leadership.
We pray for the continuity of the past with the core values You have given us.
As You have provided the seed of new life from the present we see that even in the death
of life, new spirit, new life develops.
The establishment of our Rotary club as among the vast amalgam of a worldwide
congregation of members serving mankind, provides the energy and way for us to thrive.
Where others see problems, Rotary see opportunity to serve others,
Where others see obstacles, Rotarians are energized by humanities needs for faith,
hope and charity.
As the previous administrations of our club provide the seed of new life in Rotary, we
pray that our club may flourish in the same joy You have provided for us from the past.
We thank You, Almighty God, for continuity and the continuation of Rotary tradition,
realizing that Service Above Self is serving You.
Amen.

Respect

Let us Pray;
Almighty God, heavenly father, if we may humbly request, we ask You to imbue in all
Rotarians a sense of mutual respect.
May we respect all that we serve in our community and international causes as not only
those in need, but also as individuals that You have created in Your own image. Those
who have not been able to achieve as we have, by circumstance of their environment and
personal health.
We ask, also, that we achieve respect for each other as having different gifts and motives
to achieve Rotary goals. Patience and prudence with each other, we pray, prevail
in all circumstances.
Our clubs success is based on the shared values You have given us. We incorporate these
values as Rotary ethics which we can all ascribe.
We move on from the Rotary International ideal of "Rotary Serving Humanity" to this
year. "Rotary Making a Difference"
We continuously ask the question" What is Rotary?" In deed, we have achieved our clubs
goals. Now we are guided by RI President-elect Ian H.S. Riseley's theme, *Rotary: Making
a Difference*. "Whether we're building a new playground or a new school, improving
medical care or sanitation, training conflict mediators or midwives, we know that the
work we do will change people's lives — in ways large and small — for the better."
Our unity as Rotarians processes from one year to the next with the successes designed by
our club's leadership with Your Guidance. We can only succeed by reflecting on our God
from one Rotary year to the next and pray that You may continue to be with us as we
enter a new Rotary year.
We know, that by Your grace, that respect for each other will achieve the cohesion
we need to help others.
In thy name we pray.
Amen.

Club Installation

Let us Pray
Almighty God, we thank you and praise you for all that you have given us
and our families.
As Rotarians, we thank you for guiding us through another successful year and inspiring
our Board and our President with selfless service.
We understand that our success comes from joy within our hearts to do Your will with
charity and goodwill towards others.
We pray for Your continued inspiration as we make the transition with refreshed
leadership and dedicated membership.
Amen.

Rotary as Relationships

Let us Pray!

Because "Rotary is Relationships", Rotarians are gifted with a common bond enveloped in the "Four Way Test" and our motto "Service Above Self".

We are blessed to have so many visitors to our club from so many other areas and to share family and Rotary experiences.

We praise You and thank You for all that You have given our club that we may welcome our visitors and enjoy their relationships.

We wish them Godspeed and safety in their return home.

In thy name we pray!

Amen.

Rotary by Design

From Sunrise Rotary meeting of 4/13/21 and District Conference of 4/17/21

Let us pray,

Almighty God:

You have taught us that: "a house divided against itself cannot stand".

As we see in our time an effort for the division of societal components, we understand that we cannot seek peace if we make war with each other. We pray You give us the strength to avoid anything that brings discord.

Bind us closely, as Paul Harris and his associates designed Rotary. May we remain instruments of Unity in a world torn by differences.

May our Unity of body, mind and spirit, of one heart and soul, remain with ourselves, our club and Rotary with an attitude born of charity.

We seek to be better as we imitate Your love for us, even if we see no response. By Your grace, the great Rotary tree of hope, united in charity, with our faith in You our good God, we pray to enjoy good health of spirit.

With patience and forbearance for others and an understanding of their needs, we pray to overcome all barriers and differences whether they be: social, economic, racial or cultural.

Charity, like music for the soul, unites us.

In thy name we pray.

Amen.

New Rotary Year

Let Us Pray!
Almighty God, you who oversea our efforts to change the world with our small effort.
We pray You be with our Board of Directors, as we enter a new Rotary year.
We know that each member of our board, and our President, have a major task to focus
on each and, at the same time, all of the projects we undertake.
As they present to our club a cohesive program prioritizing each program in its
importance and time, may they remember that our members support and understand the
complexity of what they do in Your name.
We pray they understand that calling on the membership to participate in what they
recommend includes Your guidance and understanding.
We are one in Your name.
Amen.

New Rotary Year

Let us Pray!
Almighty God, as we embark on a new Rotary year, we pray to recall all that You have
given us in this time of national celebration.
We pray for the same national pride and joy to be instilled in our Rotary heart that You
have given to our beloved country.
In Your infinite wisdom, we look to the gift You have given us of fresh Rotary leadership.
We pray that, with Your guidance, our new leadership may continue with Rotary pride,
enthusiasm and joy as we give to our community and world.
Amen.

Constitution

Let us Pray!
Almighty God, we, in America, have developed from the Unalienable Rights of Your
providence with the freedoms written into our Constitution.
You have blessed America with abundance well beyond what our founders envisioned.
We pray that we, as Rotarians, continue in this new Rotary year to pass on this heritage to
all the world by Service Above Self.
In thy name we pray,
Amen

Board Guidance

Let us Pray!
Almighty God, heavenly Father, we pray for unity in our Rotary club that
we may show to all that we speak and act with the same mind.
We realize that the spirit and will of our combined efforts are that much
greater than any one of us can muster.
We pray that our board of directors will continue to guide our club as
representing the thoughts of the entire body of our members and we ask
Your guidance with the members of this club to continually generate
giving projects and the revenue to fulfill Your will.
Amen.

Board Blessing

Let Us Pray!

Almighty God, you who oversea our efforts to change the world with our small effort.

We pray You be with our Board of Directors, as we enter a new Rotary year.

We know that each member of our board, and our President, have a major task to focus on each and, at the same time, all the projects we undertake.

As they present to our club a cohesive program prioritizing each program in its importance and time, may they remember that our members support and understand the complexity of what they do in Your name.

We pray they understand that calling on the membership to participate in what they recommend includes Your guidance and understanding.

We are one in Your name.

Amen.

New Leadership

Let us Pray;

We are deeply grateful, O Lord, for the gift of our great nation.

Preservation of Your ideals by us, Your people, requires constant vigilance within the framework of Your teaching.

We pray for Your guidance for our new leaders that they may respect Your principals with imminent devotion to You and the people they represent, serve and direct.

With faith, hope and charity we Rotarians pledge to set the example for all in our lives to direct Your grace to others.

Amen.

Making a Difference

Let us Pray;
Almighty God, heavenly father, as we progress into the year of "Rotary
Making a Difference" we pray for Your guidance.
We understand that one small effort by each one of us not only
contributes, but that the whole is greater than the sum of its parts.
As we contribute our time, talent and treasure to the Rotary we love, pray
that all who receive from us proceed to pass on what they have received.
May they be infused with the grace You have given Rotarians to achieve
peace in the world.
Amen.

Making a Difference

Let us Pray;
Our clubs success is based on the shared values You have given us. We incorporate
these values as Rotary ethics which we can all ascribe.
We move on from the Rotary International ideal of "Rotary Serving Humanity"
to this year. "Rotary Making a Difference"
We continuously ask the question" What is Rotary?" In deed, we have achieved our clubs
goals. Now we are guided by RI President-elect Ian H.S. Riseley's theme, Rotary: Making
a Difference. "Whether we're building a new playground or a new school, improving
medical care or sanitation, training conflict mediators or midwives, we know that the
work we do will change people's lives — in ways large and small — for the better."
Our unity as Rotarians processes from one year to the next with the successes designed by
our club's leadership with Your Guidance. We can only succeed by reflecting on our God
from one Rotary year to the next and pray that You may continue to be with us as we
enter a new Rotary year.
Amen

Grain of Sand

Let us pray,
Almighty God:
Help us to overcome the feeling that we are only one grain of sand in a
great world of needs.
Yes, we are but one grain of Rotary sand in a global network of 1.2 million
neighbors, friends, leaders, and problem-solvers who see a world where people
unite and take action to create lasting change – across the globe.
We ask You to continue to inspire Rotarians to use imagination and vision to
dedicate the variety of talents You have given us to form a beachhead against the
wave of intolerance and apathy towards our fellow citizens of the world.
As waves follow waves coming to a beach, we pray for a new great wave of
goodness, and new Rotary sand, by the building of so many missions designed to
improve the lives of those less fortunate, that we overwhelm the world in order
that evil must decline.
May each grain of sand new and old, follow Your word in a spirit of humility
and perseverance born of Your love for us.
In thy name we pray,
Amen.

Independence Day and Change of Leadership

Let us pray!
As we celebrate our nations independence we recall that we are
"One Nation Under God".
We recall all of the benefits You have given us as we are able to pursue life,
liberty and happiness.
We pray our Representative Republic always remembers why freedom is so important.
As Rotarians, we have the freedom to choose those we wish to help and pray Your grace
permits us to choose wisely.
As the "torch is passed" and our new Board takes effect, we pray that Rotary generosity
continues this year in its dedication to our areas of focus: to build international
relationships, improve lives, and create a better world to support our peace efforts and
end polio forever.
We pray for Your guidance as Rotarians project these American values for others.
In Thy name we pray!
Amen.

Guidance in the Coming Year

Let us Pray!

Almighty God, we humbly pray for Your guidance in the coming new year.
We realize that this club has been very aggressive in pursuit of goals that
challenge us every day.
We pray that our goals are just and pleasing in Your eyes that they may
ultimately bring peace and comfort to those receiving aid.
Please help us to retain the joy and discipline necessary to reach our club's
and Rotary goals and to serve others.
Amen

17. INTERNATIONAL PROJECTS

Board Guidance

Let us Pray!
Almighty God, heavenly Father, we pray for unity in our Rotary club that we may show to all that we speak and act with the same mind.
We realize that the spirit and will of our combined efforts are that much greater than any one of us can muster.
We pray that our board of directors will continue to guide our club as representing the thoughts of the entire body of our members and we ask Your guidance with the members of this club to continually generate giving projects and the revenue to fulfill Your will.
Amen.

Overriding Politics

Let us Pray;
Almighty God, one of Rotary's principal goals is
Peace and Conflict Resolution.
We pray for your guidance that we may, perhaps,
over ride political considerations as we generate
goodwill in our community and in our International
relations.
Consider our International Project in helping us to
establish that goodwill with our partner's and their
Rotary Club.
Be with us throughout, that we may all project our
heartfelt nature in this, Your Rotary world.
Amen.

18. LEADERSHIP

New Leadership

Let us Pray;
O Lord, as we gather again for our dedication to You and the cause of
giving back to our fellow citizens,
As we have Unity in our Rotary fellowship we pray for the same fidelity,
dedication and commitment in our nation.
We pray that our new leadership provide unity by the truth You provide
to help us to work with each other for the betterment of all by applying
"The Four Way Test".
We pray that all may be inspired knowing that our future rests in You
with "Service Above Self".
In thy name we pray.
Amen.

19. LOSS OF A ROTARIAN

Good and Faithful Servants

Let us Pray!

Almighty God, heavenly father. We remember and honor Your "good
and faithful servants" and cherished Rotarians who have been lost to
Sunrise Rotary in the past year:

Little needs to be said of their faithful service. We can say that they
believed in Rotary and lived Rotary principles, which are Your principles.
We pray Your indulgence and by their efforts to serve others, before
themselves, that they now reside In Your heavenly kingdom.

In thy name we pray,

Amen.

Living Legacy

Let us Pray.

Almighty God, we are in awe of the gifts You have given us.
When we lose a fellow Rotarian, we reflect and thank them for their
dedication and their service to You by selflessly participating in building
our world community to the greatness that it has become.

In the process of creation, we take You as our guide.

In the small ways we, in our humanity, participate creatively, we thank
and honor those, by Your grace, that have used their God given gifts to
think of others before themselves and give us unique pride and comfort in
our community.

Theirs is a living legacy for which we will always thank You: for their
service and inspiration.

In thy name we pray,

Amen.

20. MEALS OF HOPE

Giving Hope

Let us Pray!

Almighty God, as we consider those who are hungry in this world we pray
for your help in feeding those who need Rotary help by our small efforts.
Our local needs fulfillment has presented challenges to us with our Meals
of Hope program. We thank you for your consideration and guidance as
our club has worked our way thru this considerable process.

Please stay with us to the end we pray. May we take pride in this
accomplishment because we know You have been with us always.

Amen.

Meals of Hope

Let us pray:

Almighty God,

We become great and free and truly ourselves only when we open to You
for our inspiration and goodwill.

As Your Grace has provided for us, and as we pray for our bread, it means
that Rotarians also pray for bread for others.

To this, Rotarians take action with our "Meals of Hope" programs
because we understand that it means that Rotarians must share in the
abundance You have given us.

We pray that our efforts will, in some small measure, magnify Your glory
and inspire all to be one family.

Amen.

21. MEMBERSHIP

For Global Action

Let us pray,
Almighty God, we pray that you protect and encourage the Rotary global
network as we strive to build a world where people unite and take action
to create lasting change.
As Rotary values diversity and celebrates the contributions of people of all
backgrounds, we pray for Rotary to grow and diversify our membership to
make sure we reflect the communities we serve.
As we create an organization that is more open and inclusive, fair to all,
builds goodwill, and benefits our communities we pray for people with
differing perspectives and ideas who will help Rotary take action.
In thy name we pray,
Amen

By Your Grace

Let Us Pray!
Almighty God, You who welcome all Rotarians into your kingdom by
Your grace,
We pray we be ever mindful that each of us display that welcome to
others as members of Rotary.
We understand strangers and new members are initially reluctant as
they try to understand what Rotarians do, and the works and long
time relationships we have with each other.

We pray that their path be made easy by Your grace and our
welcoming acceptance.
Amen.

New Members

Let us pray!
As we embrace others that find in their hearts a willingness to serve others
we remember your charge to us to humbly accept all who find that
"service above self" fulfills your will.
For those that are joining Rotary efforts to serve others we wish to accept
whatever fresh and innovative help and new thinking help Rotary efforts
to improve others lives.
As a Rotary family, we pledge to work with our new members in their
interests to serve You thru Rotary.
We pray for unity of purpose and dedication to Your will for all Rotarians.
In thy name we pray,
Amen.

Vocations

Let us Pray!
Almighty God, as we approach vocations and their value in our society, we
understand that vocations bear no partiality with You.
To discern what is valuable to the individual, we pray that You guide each person to
use the best of their talent with the desire for fulfillment in their vocation.
We pray that our vocational selection may be judged by You according to our works.
Amen.

Time, Talent and Treasure

Let us Pray;
O Lord, as we gather again for our weekly dedication to You and the cause
of giving back to our fellow citizens, we recall that there are those who
have a sincere desire to give of their time, talent and treasure, but only
need the invitation to join us.
May we use Your inspiration and grace, wisely, to inspire us to fulfill
Rotary membership goals by inviting all who come before us to join in our
just cause.
In Thy name we pray.
Amen.

Good, True and Beautiful

Let us Pray!
Almighty God, You have blessed Rotarians with the resolve to preserve
and project what is good, what is true and what is beautiful.
We pray to see these blessings in all that we encounter in our work and
relationships in order to seek out opportunity to serve.
We ask for Your guidance to inquire and draw into the Rotary family all
the talent and treasure others may possess, that our service may benefit as
many as possible of those in need.
In thy name we pray,
Amen.

Rotary Projects and Programs

Let us Pray!

Almighty God, as Rotarians You have challenged us to act together and see a world where people unite and take action to create last improvement in the lives of others.

Across the globe: in our communities, and in ourselves, our neighbors and our friends, we ask for Your guidance to take action to create lasting change.

ideas, join leaders, and take action. We ask that by Your Grace, that we pour our passion, integrity, and intelligence into completing projects that have a lasting impact.

May we persevere until we deliver real, lasting solutions to create lasting change.

We pray to remember Rotary history, for more than 110 years, Rotarians have bridged cultures and connected continents to champion peace, fight illiteracy and poverty, promote clean water and sanitation, and fight disease.

We pray for Your continued grace!

Amen.

Memorium

Let us pray:

Almighty God, heavenly father we reflect on the precious gifts You have given us and resolve to protect and preserve the Rotary family.

We pause for a moment and recognize the following Rotarians lost to us as they entered Your heavenly home this past year:

(List)

These Rotarians gave of themselves that others may have a better life.

All that is good is handed down to us by the passage of family with parents providing their knowledge and Your goodness.

We pray that we may be as generous in passing on the joy and fulfillment of all that we find in Rotary.

Amen.

22. MILITARY

Preserving Freedom

Let us Pray;

O Lord, we pray first for Your guidance in the preservation of our nation as we exercise the freedom you have given us for our life, liberty and pursuit of happiness.

For those that have sacrificed so much to give us this franchise, we pray they may be remembered by all for the unselfish dedication we can only hope to emulate as Rotarians.

We pray for those left behind at home, that they may be secure in the knowledge that a grateful nation is with them in their prayers for the safe return of their loved ones.

Almighty God, protect and guide us to consider Your will be done.

Amen.

Warriors

Let us Pray!

Almighty God:

Some were Born to be Warriors

Some went to grow up.

Some because it was the only job available or, in their innocence, had a romantic notion of military life.

Whatever there need; they trained, they tired and ached, and grew into a fighting force of discipline and dedication to protect their nation.

When they joined some had the intention of protecting our liberty and at some point the rest realized that freedom wasn't free and that they were ordained to be our protectors.

By Your gracious hand they overcame fear and, with humble valor, the camaraderie that made our heroes a force became a gift of love You gave them and us.

For the memory of those that gave their lives for us and, for their sacrifice, we are grateful, Lord, for the inspiration You have given them to "Serve Above Self".

God, continue to bless America!

Amen.

Duty, Honor Country

Let us Pray!
Dear Lord, in gratitude, we are blessed by You with true heros!
Those that serve by: duty, honor, country and community.
People who day-after-day train and perform for their community what most consider
extraordinary work; but, the hero believes they are just "doing their job".
We pray that You continue to protect them. May they be clear headed in their work,
gentle and considerate in their treatment, diligent in training and performance and know
that they are loved and appreciated by a grateful community.
Amen.
Sacrifice
Let us Pray!
Almighty God, this nation thrives because of the service of our Armed Forces Veterans.
Their sacrifices have protected our freedoms, our families and our America.
We pray that this nation continue to respect and support what veterans have won in battle
against continued evolving evil.
We pray You heal those that suffer from their sacrifice.
We ask that You comfort those left behind while they defend us.
For the families of those lost, may they know, that Rotarians support and love them as
they grieve their loss.
As Rotarians pursue Peace and Conflict Resolution,
we pray for the time of judgement when: "One nation shall not raise the sword against
another, nor shall they train for war again".
In thy name we pray,
Amen.

Armed Forces Sacrifice

Let us Pray!
Almighty God, as we pass the one short day of remembering others, we pray
we do not forget the sacrifices that our Armed Forces have made for us.
Our human nature leads us on as we become absorbed in our individual lives. Please let
us take the signal from yesterday and integrate those memories into what
we do every day.
As Rotarians, our longevity as an international group of individuals and clubs doing
good, could only come from Your blessing.
Our good comes from You, and we pray that our small Rotary sacrifices may be
remembered as a gift from those who have given us our freedom through You.
Amen.

Bright White Headstones

Let us pray,
As we picture the acres of bright white headstones spanning the landscape
of our memories, let us imagine each one draped in our flag of freedom.
For those that have given their lives for our freedoms, we pause to reflect
on the shock, sorrow and grief of the parents, the wives, children and
loved ones when they learned that their warrior for freedom would no
longer be with them in person. Their grief is our own grief.
We pray to keep those who made the ultimate sacrifice alive in our
memory, and mourn with the those that were closest to them.
"A greater love hath no one than to lay down their life for a friend". But to
lay down their life for people they do not know individually, but only
knowing that they are Americans, deserves a special place in Your
Heavenly home.
In the name of those lost, we pray that their spirit live on with us, and to
paraphrase Chief Joseph of the Nez Perce Indian tribe, that someday:
"may we fight no more forever."
In thy name we pray, Amen.

Crusade

Let us Pray;
Almighty God,
With Your grace we celebrate the anniversary of the success of another
great crusade against evil.
With Your inspiration, the forces of Your good co
could only succeed in such a massive effort with Your will for all good
people to prevail against evil.
On this anniversary, Rotarians seek to emulate the dedication and sacrifice
of this great part of mankind.
We can only remember the values of courage, bravery and sacrifice taught
to us, that Rotarians in their small way, can help others to enjoy the life
that those of that great crusade have provided for us.
As we pass on the will of those that have sacrificed, and Your will for us
please continue to inspire Rotarians to build good will and greater
friendships of all.
In thy name we pray,
Amen!

Safely Bring Them Home

Let us Pray!

Lord, we thank you for all the privileges we enjoy in this great land of liberty.

We ask today for the safety of those that protect our liberty: our service men and women.

Protect them from harm as they continue to go into danger zones.

Help us to be constantly aware of their mission and high calling and bring them safely home to us.

We pray especially for those who still remain unemployed and are injured in body, mind and spirit.

Please see to their personal healing and know that we, as Rotarians, share in their tribulation.

Amen

Repatriation

Let Us Pray!

Dear God we thank you for the courageous men and women who have preserved the American way of life.

We remember the heroics and self sacrifice they have made for each of us and our families.

We pray especially for those who still remain unemployed and those that are injured in body, mind and spirit. Inspire them to become successful members of American society.

Please see to their personal healing and know that we, as Rotarians, share in their tribulation.

Amen.

Veterans

Let us Pray!
Almighty God, You have blessed Rotarians with the resolve to preserve
and project what is good, what is true and what is beautiful.
We pray to see these blessings in all that we encounter in our work and
relationships in order to seek out opportunity to serve.
We ask for Your guidance to inquire and draw into the Rotary family all
the talent and treasure others may possess, that our service may benefit as
many as possible of those in need.
In thy name we pray,
Amen.

Service Members

HOLIDAYS - 4TH OF JULY, MEMORIAL DAY, VETERANS DAY

Let us Pray;
O Lord, we pray first for Your guidance in the preservation of our nation as we exercise
the freedom you have given us for our life, liberty and pursuit of happiness.
For those that have sacrificed so much to give us this franchise, we pray they may be
remembered by all for the unselfish dedication we can only hope to emulate as Rotarians.
We pray for those left behind at home, that they may be secure in the knowledge that a
grateful nation is with them in their prayers for the safe return of their loved ones.
Almighty God, protect and guide us to consider Your will be done.
Amen.

Fortitude and Will

Let us pray;

Almighty God,

Recent events, which we judge to be both unjustified and unpunished, cannot perpetuate if our Republic is to continue and thrive on the basis of "Liberty and Justice for all".

We pray, O Lord, for the resolve to defend America against its dissolution.

We ask for Your intercession in the affairs of all by reinforcing our hearts with the fortitude and will desired by our mutual love for each other.

We pray that as Rotarians practice the building of good will, that we build a contagion of better friendships to heal the destructive practices we see.

We pray for Your grace that our link is the good we do, to create an infectious chain of good that overcomes the evil we see.

In thy name we pray,

Amen.

23. PEACE AND CONFLICT RESOLUTON

Reflection

Let us Pray!

Almighty God,

We pray to you to erase the fear and tension between people.

As Rotarians we are called to **reflect** Your infinite compassion for us and evangelize the Rotary Principal of "Peace thru Service".

As we Work to Resolve Conflict between all people, we pray to You, with sincerity of mind and purpose, for the ability to reason for ourselves and, with others, to change the hearts of those troubled souls that deny the Right to Life and Freedom.

For compassion for those oppressed and the need for order, as You have ordered the universe, we pray You give us a spirit of confidence to overcome our differences with goals and purpose for all to work to achieve life, liberty and happiness. Knowing that true peace and happiness come from serving others for You.

In thy name we pray,

Amen.

Peace and Security

Let us Pray;

Almighty God, heavenly father, we pray for the peace and security of all people.

As threats develop, we pray that You give us a singular mind to oppose oppression, poverty and suppression of individual freedom.

Give us the strength to make this a better world by "Peace thru Service". As Rotarians, the power we have is in our unity and dedication to "Service Above Self".

Help us to transmit our goals and good work in helping others to both those in need and those that wish to dominate them. That all may see that Your heavenly grace is the common denominator in achieving peace for all mankind.

In thy name we pray,

Amen.

24. PEACE THROUGH SERVICE

Is it Fair to All Concerned

Let us pray,
Almighty God,
Rotarians pledge to acknowledge and question in our daily life: Is it
"Fair to all Concerned"?
Our efforts are such as to render superficial those differences that may divide us.
You, our God, have taught us to "give unto others". We do not dwell on or wonder what
others are made of. We only need to know what are their needs. Rotarians accept our
common challenges and take refuge in the good that comes to others from our efforts.
As we go thru our daily life we pledge not to define or delineate our differences, but rather
work towards common goals and "Peace Thru Service".
Inspire in us the confidence to celebrate our diversity and inclusion.
In thy name we pray,
Amen.

With Malice Toward None

Let us pray;
Almighty God,
Two quotations come to mind:
The first: "Faith, Hope and Love. And the greatest of these is Love."
The second:
"With Malice toward none and Charity for all" as expressed in our history and in our
hearts as Americans and Rotarians.
This hope for mankind is given to us by Your grace.
The implications of Hope implies promise, but also risk and taking us out of our comfort
zone for Rotarians to advance the human condition.
Our gift is American exceptionalism and our promise is to spread the Rotary message of
hope and charity for all: with dedication and sacrifice to give unselfishly, and to perform
Your will as Faith in you gives us the comfort of hope for those in need.
As Rotarians rally together to help our fellow citizens, we remain forever in Your debt for
the inspiration to perform "Service Above Self" with a firm grip on Hope.
In thy name we pray,
Amen.

Respect for Life

Let us Pray,

Almighty God, we pray for life: dignity, "Peace thru Service" to all life. We embrace Your ideal that all human life should be respected, dignified and protected.

Rotary principals and your principals to dignify human life by its preservation thru our acts of kindness and actions tp help our fellow ----- in your name give us the enthusiasm to present Rotary programs to ensure development with clean water, food and basic human needs.

We understand that you are in charge of the beginnings of life and that we can only work for your ideals in life's development after birth. May our minor efforts find favor with You by providing for others needs.

In thy name we pray,

Amen

Right to Life

Let us Pray!

Almighty God,

We pray to you to erase the fear and tension between people.

As Rotarians we are called to **reflect** Your infinite compassion for us and evangelize the Rotary Principal of "Peace thru Service".

As we Work to Resolve Conflict between all people, we pray to You, with sincerity of mind and purpose, for the ability to reason for ourselves and, with others, to change the hearts of those troubled souls that deny the Right to Life and Freedom.

For compassion for those oppressed and the need for order, as You have ordered the universe, we pray You give us a spirit of confidence to overcome our differences with goals and purpose for all to work to achieve life, liberty and happiness. Knowing that true peace and happiness come from serving others for You.

In thy name we pray,

Amen.

Common Good

Let us pray,
Almighty God, Heavenly Father
we pray as we maintain communion with each other in common cause and take
inspiration from our motto: "Service Above Self".
As our Communion of Rotary like minds and spirit are being tested, as are all those
subject to severe health concerns, we take solace knowing
You have given us the ability to adapt creatively to socially distance ourselves from each
other. We know that You are with us in communion without distance.
As we endeavor to embrace all those with health hardships and, as we make the best of the
Burden of Separation from each other, we reflect on not being separated from You. We
gather inspiration and hope
as we muster Rotarian talents and abilities to persevere under difficult circumstances. Our
hope in communion with You can only make Rotarians stronger in our dedication for
"Peace thru Service".
In thy name we pray,
Amen.

Leadership

Let us Pray!
Almighty God, we praise you and thank you for providing Rotary with
giving Rotarians and those who look to you for counsel as our leaders.
Where there is hunger and poverty there are Rotarians.
Where there is weather disasters there are Rotarians.
Where education is needed there are Rotarians.
Where health problems exist Rotarians volunteer.
Conflict resolution causes Rotarians to volunteer because we believe in
"Peace thru Service".

We continue to pray for Your guidance to our leadership that all may
enjoy the love You inspire.
Amen

25. PROTECT AND SERVE

Preserving Order

Let us pray!
Almighty God, heavenly father we pray for those that protect us and serve to make sure that our order is preserved.
We are thankful for the extreme dedication they possess with the motivation to train constantly that we may enjoy the American way of life in peace and security.
We pray for their safety as they go into harms way to assure our safety.
Be with them, O Lord, knowing that we, those that they serve, are thankful for their dedication to us and to their families.
Amen.

"Service Above Self"

Let us pray;
Almighty God, we praise you and thank you for our public servants. Folks that train and work for others in need everyday performing "Service Above Self".
We thank our first responders for always being present to sacrifice in emergency, but also being ever-present in our community for assistance as needed.
Our public servants first respond to our call and volunteer their time, facilities and equipment to enhance our welfare and sense of community experience. Our first responders bring public service to a higher level and bring the community together in the a spirit of Your love for us.
We pray, as a community of Rotarians, that in this season of salvation and love for each other, their service becomes an inspiration for the next generation to serve.
In thy name we pray,
Amen.

Be Not Afraid

Let us pray;
Almighty God, our hope is in you.
We take to heart your abundant grace and invocation to
"Be not afraid". In our time of crisis, in this period of our isolation from one another, we pray to continue our Rotary mission of improving health and disease prevention in a troubled world.
We pray for those in need of the hope that You provide. Take those who succumb to disease into Your heavenly home.
May those that become infected be imbued with the hope and optimism that faith in You provide for their healing.
For caregivers, who selflessly put themselves in harms way, we pray that You help them maintain their sense of mission with dedication and enthusiasm because they have the ability to inspire all.
As we take measures to meet our mission, we pray to use collective Rotary minds and intellect to find ways to communicate mission as a great challenge. In this time of crisis we pray for the enthusiasm to stick to our cause.
As your humble servants, we understand that communication through our prayer to You is the greatest communication.
In thy name we pray,
Amen.

Self Sacrifice

Let us Pray,
Almighty God, our hope and refuge, in our distress we come quickly to You.
We are mindful of the sacrifice of public servants who demonstrate the greatest love of all by sacrificing their well being for friends and many who they didn't know at all.
Using their example, we come remembering and we come in hope, not in ourselves, but in You and the unity of Rotary.
We do not disguise our belief. Help us to project Rotary and what Rotary stands for to all that we come in contact.
Help us to put aside our differences and concerns as we welcome others to join Rotary.
We pray to project Your spirit as Rotary's spirit of giving and service to: "the least of these our brethren".
In thy name we pray,
Amen.

Maintaining Order

Let us Pray!
Almighty God, heavenly father we pray for those that protect us and serve to make sure that our order and lives are preserved.
We are thankful for the extreme dedication they possess with the motivation to train constantly that we may enjoy the American way of life in peace and security.
We pray for their safety as they go into harms way to assure our safety, and that we, as Rotarians and citizens, find the courage to perform with fidelity as their guidance requires.
Be with them, O Lord, knowing that we, those that they serve, are thankful for their dedication to us and to their families.
Amen.

In our Distress

Let us Pray,
Almighty God, our hope and refuge, in our distress we come quickly to You.
We are mindful of the sacrifice of public servants who demonstrate the greatest love of all by sacrificing their well being for friends and many who they didn't know at all.
Using their example, we come remembering and we come in hope, not in ourselves, but in You and the unity of Rotary.
We do not disguise our belief. Help us to project Rotary and what Rotary stands for to all that we come in contact.
Help us to put aside our differences and concerns as we welcome others to join Rotary. We pray to project Your spirit as Rotary's spirit of giving and service to: "the least of these our brethren".
In thy name we pray,
Amen.

Headstones

Let us pray,
As we picture the acres of bright white headstones spanning the landscape of our
memories, let us imagine each one draped in our flag of freedom.
For those that have given their lives for our freedoms, we pause to reflect on the shock,
sorrow and grief of the parents, the wives, children and loved ones when they learned that
their warrior for freedom would no longer be with them in person. Their grief is
our own grief.
We pray to keep those who made the ultimate sacrifice alive in our memory, and mourn
with the those that were closest to them.
"A greater love hath no one than to lay down their life for a friend". But to lay down their
life for people they do not know individually, but only knowing that they are Americans,
deserves a special place in Your Heavenly home.
In the name of those lost, we pray that their spirit live on with us, and to paraphrase Chief
Joseph of the Nez Perce Indian tribe, that someday: "may we fight no more forever."
In thy name we pray,
Amen.

Voluntary

Let us pray;
Almighty God, we praise you and thank you for our public servants. Folks that train and
work for others in need everyday performing "Service Above Self".
We thank our first responders for always being present to sacrifice in emergency, but also
being ever-present in our community for assistance as needed.
Our public servants first respond to our call and volunteer their time, facilities and
equipment to enhance our welfare and sense of community experience. Our first
responders bring public service to a higher level and bring the community together in the
a spirit of Your love for us.
We pray, as a community of Rotarians, that in this season of salvation and love for each
other, their service becomes an inspiration for the next generation to serve.
In thy name we pray,
Amen.

First Responders

Let us pray,
We thank our first responders for always being present to sacrifice in emergency,
but also being ever-present in our community for assistance as needed.
Our public servants first respond to our call and volunteer their time, facilities and
equipment to enhance our welfare and sense of community experience. Our first
responders bring public service to a higher level and bring the community
together in the a spirit of Your love for us.
We pray, as a community of Rotarians, that in this season of salvation and love for
each other, their service becomes an inspiration for the next generation to serve.
In thy name we pray,
Amen.

First Responders

Let us pray.
Almighty God, heavenly father,
We praise You and thank You for giving us dedicated public servants. Those that
serve to protect our lives and property.
The natural consequences of the evolution of the world that You have created,
that put us in occasional harms way, require Your grace to inspire their dedication
to protecting others.
We do not wish for tragedy for anyone. If and when it occurs, we rest in assurance
that responders act with Your inspiration to protect Your people.
For those that give us security, we pray that their judgement and energy be
inspired by You.
In thy name we pray,
Amen.

No Greater Love

Let us pray,
As we picture the acres of bright white headstones spanning the landscape
of our memories, let us imagine each one draped in our flag of freedom.
For those that have given their lives for our freedoms, we pause to reflect
on the shock, sorrow and grief of the parents, the wives, children and
loved ones when they learned that their warrior for freedom would no
longer be with them in person. Their grief is our own grief.
We pray to keep those who made the ultimate sacrifice alive in our
memory, and mourn with the those that were closest to them.
"A greater love hath no one than to lay down their life for a friend". But to
lay down their life for people they do not know individually, but only
knowing that they are Americans, deserves a special place in Your
Heavenly home.
In the name of those lost, we pray that their spirit live on with us, and to
paraphrase Chief Joseph of the Nez Perce Indian tribe, that someday:
"may we fight no more forever."
In thy name we pray,
Amen.

26. PUBLIC SERVICE

Community

Let us Pray,
Almighty God, we praise You and thank You for providing us with this
wonderful world and beautiful community.
We pray for Your grace in protecting our citizens that they may be guided
by our elected officials and public servants. Always knowing that You
have provided us with life, liberty and the pursuit of happiness.
Our environment is a gift from You, and we pray for official guidance in
the protection of what we have that inspires us to be part of this
community.
In Thy name we pray,
Amen.

First Responders

Let us pray.
Almighty God, heavenly father,
We praise You and thank You for giving us dedicated public servants.
Those that serve to protect our lives and property.
The natural consequences of the evolution of the world that You have
created, that put us in occasional harms way, require Your grace to inspire
their dedication to protecting others.
We do not wish for tragedy for anyone. If and when it occurs, we rest in
assurance that responders act with Your inspiration tprotect Your people.
For those that give us security, we pray that their judgement and energy be
inspired by You.
In thy name we pray,
Amen.

Heros

Let us Pray!
Dear Lord, in gratitude, we are blessed by You with true heros!
Those that serve by: duty, honor, country and community.
People who day-after-day train and perform for their community what most consider
extraordinary work; but, the hero believes they are just "doing their job".
We pray that You continue to protect them. May they be clear headed in their work,
gentle and considerate in their treatment, diligent in training and performance and know
that they are loved and appreciated by a grateful community.
Amen.

Unsung Hero

Let us pray:
Songs are sung of hero's past, of those distinguished in battle, or elevated
to great position.
But what of the great mass of mankind who, by God's grace, performed with valor, honor
and without the glory of worldly recognition.
Those that did what had to be done in their time and in a way that gives glory to God:
unselfish and tempered by their time. Those unsung.
They live today, in a different way, a different place, as warriors in public service and are
spontaneous in doing right in a time of crisis.
They have learned to do right sometimes by how they were brought up and then through
training. They live among us.
Respect and honor. Unselfish. Hero's are not to be worshiped, they do not care to be
worshiped. If ego exists in the hero, question whether they are hero's?
Duty, honor, country, community.
They live where dedication to duty is distinctive and valor is common.
Where their working realm is a zone apart, not to be pierced by outside thought.
The hero mocks the self proclaimed by his humility, his simple act of not reacting in his
own self interest. He does not proclaim he is the greatest, the best. Those
that are self adorned.
His cause is not himself.
The hero does and walks away. He hides in the comfort of duty performed.
A hero is dedicated, singleminded, other worldly, without thought for themselves. Hero is
not the way they think. They pass on what they believe by their actions. We wish we could
be like them. Their belief system is spontaneous because of training, dedication, duty,
honor, country, community.
Their glory is in You, our God.
In thy name we pray,
Amen.

27. STEWARDSHIP

Environment

Let us pray;

Almighty God!

As Rotarians we seek what is good, what is true and what is beautiful.

We reflect on the magnificent beauty in the world you have given us.

Rotarians pledge to protect and balance the beauty of Your Creation with the needs of mankind and the depletion of resources which occurs for our progress.

You have given us Stewardship over our environment with the freedom to fruitfully care for its majesty.

We pray for Your continued guidance to perform what is true and good in Your eyes.

In thy name we pray!

Amen.

Making a Difference

Let us Pray;

Almighty God, heavenly father, as we progress into the year of "Rotary Making a Difference" we pray for Your guidance.

We understand that one small effort by each one of us not only contributes, but that the whole is greater than the sum of its parts.

As we contribute our time, talent and treasure to the Rotary we love, pray that all who receive from us proceed to pass on what they have received.

May they be infused with the grace You have given Rotarians to achieve peace in the world.

Amen.

American Ideals

Let Us Pray!

Almighty God, we are forever grateful for the infusion of Your and American principles of Liberty, Justice and the industry to pass on to all the world these ideals through Rotary.

We thank You for providing us with the ability to work, with Your Grace, and give others incentive by helping them to improve their lives.

The infection of Your principals provide American Rotarians with necessary pride to perpetuate giving to others and dedicate each Club to make this a better world by our service.

Amen.

28. TRAGEDY

Memorium

Let us Pray;
Almighty God, we praise you and thank you for your everlasting care. Thy will be done.
As a nation in mourning, we are coming to terms with horrific tragedy close to us
and pray to understand.
As You, our God, knows the plan You have established, we pray to believe and
understand that whatever occurs in our world on Earth has a glorious future for those
who believe in You.
We pray for the souls who perish through evil. May you take them into
your heavenly kingdom.
We pray for consolation in the hearts of those who are closest to those perished with
reconciliation and recognition of You in Your infinite wisdom.
Theirs is a living legacy for which we will always thank You: for their service and
inspiration.
Amen.

Let us Pray;
Almighty God, we praise you and thank you for your everlasting care. Thy will be done.
As a nation in mourning, we are coming to terms with horrific tragedy in the mid-west
and pray to understand.
As You, our God, knows the plan You have established, we pray to believe and
understand that whatever occurs in our world on Earth has a glorious future for those
who believe in You.
We pray for the souls who perish through these sudden events. May you take them into
your heavenly kingdom.
We pray for consolation in the hearts of those who are closest to those perished with
reconciliation and recognition of You in Your infinite wisdom.
We pray for those who serve to re-establish the living conditions of communities
tragically degraded and lost. As Rotarians assist in these efforts we ask for Your grace.
Theirs is a living legacy for which we will always thank You: for their service and
inspiration.
Amen.

Consolation

Let us Pray;
Almighty God, heavenly father, we praise You and thank You for sending
us good and faithful servants.
As we celebrate today those you have taken into Your heavenly home, we pray to
remember their deeds and accomplishments in their acts of Sainthood.
We pray to follow in their unmentioned and undesired fame as Rotarians dedicated to
serving others in our community and Your world.
We pray for Your guidance in all our projects that Rotarians be known as givers desiring
no credit for their work.
Amen.

Legacy

Let is Pray;
Almighty God, heavenly father, we pray for the care of those who have preceded us in life.
As we remember their example and contributions
to our society we pray that You protect and prolong their life, with quality, as they
proceed to You in their heavenly home.
For those that dedicate themselves to the care of those passing through life, we pray for
their continued passion in passing on Your empathy and love.
Amen.

Losing a Brother

Let us Pray!

We are in awe of the gifts You have given us.

When we lose a brother, we reflect and thank those that have dedicated their lives and have continued to serve You, our community and ourselves by selflessly participating in building our community from the beginning to the greatness that it has become.

In the process of creation, we take You as our guide. In the small ways we, in our humanity, participate in creativity we thank and honor those, by Your grace, that have used their creative ability to think of others before themselves and give us the unique pride and comfort of our community.

In thy name we pray,

Amen.

Decline

Let us Pray!

Almighty God and father of all, as Rotarians we continue to experience the decline of our loved ones.

We do pray for their recovery and realize their slow departure from us and their welcome by You.

We pray for those that see to their welfare and show with loving care respect as they share in their memories together.

As a family of Rotarians, we pray to share with the caregivers among us their loving experience.

In Thy name we pray,

Amen.

911 Memorial

Let us pray,
Almighty God, As we approach yet another anniversary of tragedy and evil perpetrated against others in humanity we remember all those lost and pray they are now in Your care.
For those we knew who perished on 9/11/2001, let us now recall their names and their families:

I remember: _____

Anyone else? _____

For all those lost and those left to grieve we pray for Your consolation in helping them heal.
We praise You, Almighty God, for those that sacrificed and who gave of themselves to prove the heroism and goodwill in helping heal the great wound created.
Rotarians pray for Peace and Resolution of Conflicts. Please protect us, O God, from all those who wish to inflict harm on others. May Rotarians become the engine of a world at peace.
In thy name we pray,
Amen.

911 Memorial

Let us pray,
Almighty God, It is appropriate today that Rotarians dwell on the tragic lose of our youth with a brutal attack on our country and how we can honor their memory. With their exuberant youth they chose to serve - as Rotarians choose to serve.
By Your will, we pray now for vigilance against forces of evil and dedicate ourselves to serving new generations as **our** means of strengthening our nation and community.
To those lost as they honored our country and us, they performed their Duty with a courage born of the values You have given to all mankind. We pray, our God, with our hope in You, to emulate that courage and valor with **our** service to perpetuate their memory.
Thru Rotary programs such as Interact, Rotaract, Youth Exchange, S4TL, training and education, we pray for Your guidance as Rotarians salute those lost by educating generations succeeding us.
In thy name we pray,
Amen.

911 Memorial

Let us pray,
Almighty God, It is appropriate today that Rotarians dwell on the tragic lose of our youth
with a brutal attack on our country and how we can honor their memory. With their
exuberant youth they chose to serve - as Rotarians choose to serve.
By Your will, we pray now for vigilance against forces of evil and dedicate ourselves to
serving new generations as our means of strengthening our nation and community.
To those lost as they honored our country and us, they performed their Duty with a
courage born of the values You have given to all mankind. We pray, our God, with our
hope in You, to emulate that courage and valor with our service to perpetuate
their memory.
Thru Rotary programs such as Interact, Rotaract, Youth Exchange, S4TL, training and
education, we pray for Your guidance as Rotarians salute those lost by educating
generations succeeding us.
In thy name we pray,
Amen.

Empathy for Others

Let us pray!
As we make our way through this life we sometimes need to be awakened from our own
problems to finally realize that we long to see your face and are not alone.
As we are accustomed to our comfortable life in paradise, there are others, Rotarians work
to reach, that require assistance for the very basics in life.
As we practice to understand their plight we ask for Your guidance and grace
to truly understand their needs.
We pray that Rotarians work in harmony that we may assist those in need.
In thy name we pray!
Amen

Personal Tragedy

Let us Pray!
We all feel the pain of tragedy to our fellow man and often wonder why
bad things happen to good people.
As Rotarians we see many tragedies and conflicts in Your world that we can only offer
our small part in making life easier and worthwhile for those in need.
There is no satisfaction in tragedy and we pray that there be some consolation for the
victims and their loved ones in knowing that others are thinking and praying
for their healing.
Bad things happen and we recognize that You, our God, is with us in promoting the
good and beauty by unifying us in the knowledge of Your loving kindness to all.
In thy name we pray,
Amen.

Nation in Mourning

Let us Pray!
Almighty God, we praise you and thank you for your everlasting care.
Thy will be done.
As a nation in mourning, we are coming to terms with horrific tragedy close to us
and pray to understand.
As You, our God, knows the plan You have established, we pray to believe and
understand that whatever occurs in our world on Earth has a glorious future for
those who believe in You.
We pray for the souls who perish through evil. May you take them into your
heavenly kingdom.
We pray for consolation in the hearts of those who are closest to those perished
with reconciliation and recognition of You in Your infinite wisdom.
Amen.

Natural Disaster

Let us pray!

Almighty God, heavenly father we are extremely thankful for the grace You have bestowed on us. We are thankful that the extreme destruction of our precious island did not occur.

We are thankful for the inspiration and dedication of those who respond with necessary services.

As we adjust to the calamities our community has experienced, we pray for Your continued grace as we recover.

We pray to remember those less fortunate to bring their lives back to normal. The struggle they pursue is perhaps more severe than our own.

We pray that the giving nature of Rotarians in our community remain an inspiration to all.

In thy name we pray!

Amen.

Anniversary Day (District Meeting 5/13/18)

Let us pray!

This is a day we remember as a horror for the loss of so many worthy souls innocently taken from us.

In their innocence, however, their sacrifice has given us unity in Your name. The determination shown in the recovery from the evil is worthy of all that You have given us as a people and reinforces the Rotary principal of: Service Above Self".

We pray that as we remember the events of that day and the loss of our friends, we may continue to perform as Rotarians in unity with all that suffered loss on that day.

In thy name we pray!

Amen.

Personal

Let us Pray!
We all feel the pain of tragedy to our fellow man and often wonder why
bad things happen to good people.
As Rotarians we see many tragedies and conflicts in Your world that we
can only offer our small part in making life easier and worthwhile for
those in need.
There is no satisfaction in tragedy and we pray that there be some
consolation for the victims and their loved ones in knowing that others are
thinking and praying for their healing.
Bad things happen and we recognize that You, our God, is with us in
promoting the good and beauty by unifying us in the knowledge of Your
loving kindness to all.
In thy name we pray,
Amen.

29. UNITY

Club Unity

Let us Pray!
Almighty God, heavenly Father, we pray for unity in our Rotary club that
we may show to all that we speak and act with the same mind.
We realize that the spirit and will of our combined efforts are that much
greater than any one of us can muster.
We pray that our board of directors will continue to guide our club as
representing the thoughts of the entire body of our members and we ask
Your guidance with the members of this club to continually generate
giving projects and the revenue to fulfill Your will.
Amen.

A House Divided

From Sunrise Rotary meeting of 4/13/21 and District Conference of 4/17/21

Let us pray,
Almighty God:
You have taught us that: "a house divided against itself cannot stand".
As we see in our time an effort for the division of societal components, we understand
that we cannot seek peace if we make war with each other. We pray You give us the
strength to avoid anything that brings discord.
Bind us closely, as Paul Harris and his associates designed Rotary. May we remain
instruments of Unity in a world torn by differences.
May our Unity of body, mind and spirit, of one heart and soul,
remain with ourselves, our club and Rotary with an attitude born of charity.
We seek to be better as we imitate Your love for us, even if we see no response. By Your
grace, the great Rotary tree of hope, united in charity, with our faith in You our good
God, we pray to enjoy good health of spirit.
With patience and forbearance for others and an understanding of their needs, we pray to
overcome all barriers and differences whether they be: social, economic, racial or cultural.
Charity, like music for the soul, unites us.
In thy name we pray.
Amen.

Respect

Let us Pray;
Almighty God, heavenly father, if we may humbly request, we ask You to imbue in all
Rotarians a sense of mutual respect.
May we respect all that we serve in our community and international causes as not only those
in need, but also as individuals that You have created in Your own image. Those who have not
been able to achieve as we have, by circumstance of their environment
and personal health.
We ask, also, that we achieve respect for each other as having different gifts and motives to
achieve Rotary goals. Patience and prudence with each other, we pray, prevail in all
circumstances.
Our clubs success is based on the shared values You have given us. We incorporate these
values as Rotary ethics which we can all ascribe.
We move on from the Rotary International ideal of "Rotary Serving Humanity" to this year.
"Rotary Making a Difference"
We continuously ask the question" What is Rotary?" In deed, we have achieved our clubs
goals. Now we are guided by RI President-elect Ian H.S. Riseley's theme, *Rotary: Making a
Difference.* "Whether we're building a new playground or a new school, improving medical
care or sanitation, training conflict mediators or midwives, we know that the work we do will
change people's lives — in ways large and small — for the better."
Our unity as Rotarians processes from one year to the next with the successes designed by our
club's leadership with Your Guidance. We can only succeed by reflecting on our God from
one Rotary year to the next and pray that You may continue to be with us as we enter a new
Rotary year.
We know, that by Your grace, that respect for each other will achieve the cohesion
we need to help others.
In thy name we pray.
Amen.

Four Way Test

Let us pray,
Rotarians follow the four way test: we understand that to build goodwill and better friendships
we must be together. It is this together unity that dynamically produces benefits to all.
Our separation has caused us to adapt and pursue other means of communication and
dedication to the Rotary cause. We have, at last, slipped the surly bonds of separation from
each other. We can now gather and enjoy each others company to hear and evaluate the
concerns and needs of the greater community in a direct way.
You have given Your people the power of knowledge and intellect to fulfill Your mission of
coming together. We worship You, the God of all, because our intellect directs us to the cause
of charity for those in need. We pray that the sounding board of direct contact with each will
enjoin our spirits as a mutual Rotary spirit to work in Your name.
In thy name we pray,
Amen.

Global Network

Let us pray,

Almighty God, we pray that you protect and encourage the Rotary global network as we strive to build a world where people unite and take action to create lasting change.
As Rotary values diversity and celebrates the contributions of people of all backgrounds, we pray for Rotary to grow and diversify our membership to make sure we reflect the communities we serve.
As we create an organization that is more open and inclusive, fair to all, builds goodwill, and benefits our communities we pray for people with differing perspectives and ideas who will help Rotary take action.
In thy name we pray,
Amen

Conquering Disease

Let us pray -

Almighty God, It is that time, at calendar yearend, that we account for the blessings You have given us.
Many of Your people have experienced great trial and tribulation. We take comfort in knowing that You, our God, are there for council and hope.
Thru it all You have given us the intellect and drive to persevere and eventually conquer a devastating disease.
As we reflect the true spirit of Rotary in a greater way in life, we ask for Your continued guidance. We pray to reflect on Your will for Your people.
We pray to bring Rotary strength thru unity as we do Your work. Unity is rotary's strength. With dedication, measured reflection and care, as we enter a new calendar year, we ask You to continue to bless Rotarians and our programs, as we adapt, modify our actions and programs to meet new challenges.
In thy name we pray,
Amen.

30. VISITING ROTARIANS

Fellowship

Let us Pray;
Almighty God, we thank You and praise You for blessing us with Rotarian
visitors to our club.
As they add to our fellowship and energy we can only thank You for their
giving attitude to enhance a common belief in Rotary principals.
We pray that as they leave us, that they travel in safety and bring back to
their home clubs a sense of who we all are as Rotarians.
In thy name we pray.
Amen.

Relationships

Let us Pray!
Because "Rotary is Relationships", Rotarians are gifted with a common bond
enveloped in the "Four Way Test" and our motto "Service Above Self".
We are blessed to have so many visitors to our club from so many other areas and
to share family and Rotary experiences.
We praise You and thank You for all that You have given our club that we may
welcome our visitors and enjoy their relationships.
We wish them Godspeed and safety in their return home.
In thy name we pray!
Amen.

31. YOUTH

Children's Health

Let us Pray;
Almighty God, we thank You and pray to You for the health and safety of our children.
As Rotarians continue to give to causes to improve the lives of those generations
following, we ask for Your blessing on their efforts for self development. We also ask that
You continue to protect them in development of a health body, mind and spirit.
Rotarians continue to provide scholarships for their education. Rotarians seek to improve
children's health by eliminating disease and create good health habits. We turn to You to
instill in our children the spirit to develop Rotarian values and then pass on this,
Your will, for all.
Our cause is Your cause. Give us the will to sacrifice what is necessary in the development
of future generations.
In thy name we pray,
Amen.

Programs

Let us pray,
Almighty God, As we recall that day almost 80 years ago that America was brutally
attacked without warning, our nation lost young people of principal and dedication.
By Your will, we pray now for vigilance against forces of evil and dedicate ourselves to
serving new generations as our means of strengthening our nation and community.
To those lost as they honored our country and us, they performed their Duty with a
courage born of the values You have given to all mankind. We pray, our God, to emulate
that courage and valor with our service.
Thru Rotary programs such as RLI, Youth Exchange,
S4TL, training and education, we pray for Your guidance as Rotarians salute those lost by
educating generations succeeding us.
In thy name we pray,
Amen.

Children in Harm's Way

Let us Pray!
Almighty God, we pray for all children in harms way.
We ask Your intercession to rescue children that are at risk for survival
and are at the disposal of natural events.
For those that are actively involved in rescue efforts we pray that their
training and expertise may give them the motivation and dedication to
persevere and insure the safety of children.
As Rotarians, we pray that Your love envelop us to make sure that all
children can become good citizens and overcome conflict, disease, lack of
nutrition and poverty.
In Thy name we pray!
Amen.

God Parents

Let us Pray!
As Rotarians, we understand that we are the God parents of Rotaract,
Interact and Rotary Kids.
Almighty God, we pray for Your guidance in directing with joyful
dedication the Rotary programs that mirror our own family.
Fidelity to You by mentoring with Rotary principals and values as we
would in our own families.
We pray for Your guidance in using our resources of experience and
knowledge with compassion and wisdom, to project all that You have
given us - as Rotarians.
Amen.

Caregivers

Let us pray!
Almighty God, heavenly father we pray for the health and welfare of our children.
We pray that all parents take the responsibility and be inspired with the love and
faith You have given us to dedicate to future generations.
We pray that caregivers, teachers and child advocates nurture and protect
those in their care.
We pray that children may develop childhood memories making them good
citizens and, as Your children, that they project that image to future generations.
In thy name we pray!
Amen.

Health and Safety

Let us Pray;
Almighty God, we thank You and pray to You for the health and
safety of our children.
As Rotarians continue to give to causes to improve the lives of those
generations following, we ask for Your blessing on their efforts for self
development. We also ask that You continue to protect them in
development of a health body, mind and spirit.
Rotarians continue to provide scholarships for their education. Rotarians
seek to improve children's health by eliminating disease and create good
health habits. We turn to You to instill in our children the spirit to develop
Rotarian values and then pass on this Your will, for all.
Our cause is Your cause. Give us the will to sacrifice what is necessary in
the development of future generations.
In thy name we pray,
Amen.

Interact, RYLA, S4TL

Let us Pray!
Lord, You who have given us the gifts of discernment and discretion to conduct our Rotary and everyday lives - protect our youth and their caregivers.
Work through us to prudently discover the goodness in others and especially in our youth.
We pray that Your reward, and gift of the Holy Spirit, be with those who selflessly give of their talents and treasures for the betterment of our youth in our community and for a world of Rotarian principals.
Amen.

Interact, RYLA, Youth Exchange, S4TL, Dictionary

Let us Pray;
Almighty God, heavenly father of good council,
You, who came as a teacher for all mankind and revealed that true teaching is from the will of God.
We praise You and thank You for the education we and our families have received and, as Rotarians, pledge Rotary's core Area of Focus for Basic Education and Literacy for everyone to promote Peace and Conflict Resolution.
We ask You to bless our own Good Will thru education: RYLA, Youth Exchange, S4TL, Interact, the Dictionary Program and our Scholarship Program.
Give us the wisdom to discern and to promote these programs as we demonstrate Your teaching to us.
Amen.

Interact, Rotary Kids, RYLA,S4TL

Let us Pray!

Almighty God, we appreciate the insight that Rotary has given us to work with the exchange of youth, with their fresh thinking and open mind.

We enjoy the opportunity to understand future cooperation and development, and invest in the interest of those we previously knew little about.

As we wash away prejudice for other cultures and encourage unity of heart and mind, we pray for Your continued guidance as new ideas from those we may have held previous differences, are revealed.

In thy name we pray.

Amen!

Rotaract, Interact and Rotary Kids

Let us Pray!

As Rotarians, we understand that we are the God parents of Rotaract, Interact and Rotary Kids.

Almighty God, we pray for Your guidance in directing with joyful dedication the Rotary programs that mirror our own family.

Fidelity to You by mentoring with Rotary principals and values as we would in our own families.

We pray for Your guidance in using our resources of experience and knowledge with compassion and wisdom, to project all that You have given us - as Rotarians.

Amen.

Pearl Harbor

Let us pray,
Almighty God, As we recall that day almost 80 years ago that America was brutally attacked without warning, our nation lost young people of principal and dedication. By Your will, we pray now for vigilance against forces of evil and dedicate ourselves to serving new generations as our means of strengthening our nation and community. To those lost as they honored our country and us, they performed their Duty with a courage born of the values You have given to all mankind. We pray, our God, to emulate that courage and valor with our service.
Thru Rotary programs such as RLI, Youth Exchange,
S4TL, training and education, we pray for Your guidance as Rotarians salute those lost by educating generations succeeding us.
In thy name we pray,
Amen.

Scouting

Let Us Pray!
Almighty God, You have endowed our youth leadership with qualities that prepare young people for life and the ability to take action in a static and dynamic society.
"Semper Quisitum Cuelo." Always seek heaven.
Scouting teaches qualities to be: trustworthy, loyal, helpful, friendly, courteous, kind, obedient to the grace You provide, cheerful, thrifty, brave, clean and reverent.
By putting youth in the middle of action and encouraging them to succeed, the immediate merit rewards provides them with the building blocks to succeed in adult life and career by putting service above self.
In Thy name we pray,
Amen.

Tragedy

Let us pray,

Almighty God, It is appropriate today that Rotarians dwell on the tragic lose of our youth with a brutal attack on our country and how we can honor their memory. With their exuberant youth they chose to serve - as Rotarians choose to serve.

By Your will, we pray now for vigilance against forces of evil and dedicate ourselves to serving new generations as **our** means of strengthening our nation and community.

To those lost as they honored our country and us, they performed their Duty with a courage born of the values You have given to all mankind. We pray, our God, with our hope in You, to emulate that courage and valor with their service to perpetuate their memory.

Thru Rotary programs such as Interact, Rotaract, Youth Exchange, S4TL, training and education, we pray for Your guidance as Rotarians salute those lost by educating generations succeeding us.

In thy name we pray,

Amen.

Made in the USA
Las Vegas, NV
09 January 2025

16086314R00134